Creating
Abundance

Creating Abundance

HOW TO BRING WEALTH AND FULFILMENT INTO YOUR LIFE

Andrew Ferguson

PIATKUS

© 1992 Andrew Ferguson

First published in 1992 by
Judy Piatkus (Publishers) Ltd
5 Windmill Street, London W1P 1HF

The moral right of the author has been asserted

*A catalogue record for this book is
available from the British Library*

ISBN 0-7499-1173-5

Edited by Carol Franklin
Designed by Paul Saunders
Cover by Jennie Smith

Set in Compugraphic Palatino by
Action Typesetting Ltd, Gloucester
Printed and bound in Great Britain by
Mackays of Chatham PLC

Contents

1

The Age of Abundance

THE Age of Abundance is a feeling, a belief system, an altered state of consciousness. It is not a lost Golden Age, nor a New Era just arriving. It has always existed and will always exist. All we have to do is acknowledge it, and then we will have entered it.

There are many routes by which one may arrive in the Age of Abundance. We might have discovered it during the Industrial Age. The founders of that age certainly thought so and were motivated by the prospect of fair shares for all, and an end to drudgery and disease. But the dream turned sour. Now with recession and collapse in the North, and devastation in the South, it is still possible to enter the Age of Abundance. We failed to learn the lesson and acknowledge our abundance during the years of prosperity. Now we are being offered a last chance, to discover it during an economic downturn. Paradoxically, abundance is more readily accessible in the bad times than during a short-lived artificial boom.

MONEY IS DEAD: LONG LIVE ABUNDANCE

There is never enough money or prosperity to create abundance. We know this. We have tried it. We in the West have created and accumulated vast wealth, and all it has generated is fear of losing it and a desire for even more wealth, more conquests and more growth at the expense of others. With prosperity there are always winners and losers. Yet even the winners, those who succeed most by the old standards, do not appear to have discovered a feeling of abundance or fulfilment, but keep seeking more and more instead.

The old ways of winning carry a high price – loss of authenticity and freedom, compromising values, not doing what one really wants to do, not ever *being*. At the end of it all, there may be wealth, but there will rarely be more than a shallow happiness. As times get tougher, it becomes harder to achieve even these superficial rewards and fewer people make it, or feel they can make it. So more and more people question whether it is worth making concessions. Being a cardboard cut-out doesn't work: why not try being yourself? As the prospect of wealth diminishes, the reluctance to come off the tracks and adopt a more real approach to life dies too. The end of false prosperity marks the beginning of the path to abundance – appreciating what we have, valuing life, caring for what we believe, following our bliss.

Hard times help us discover abundance. A job is no longer a guarantee of adequate income. A house may be worth less than we paid for it. A pile of money may become worthless overnight. Without a belief in abundance, there can only be despair. And now none of the old symbols of security that imprisoned us have any worth or validity, our search elsewhere is bound to intensify. Now is the time to enter the Age of Abundance.

OUT OF THE NURSERY

The door is ajar. It's actually been like that for a very long time. There have just been so many other preoccupations, that it has not been a priority to investigate further. And it's a little frightening. Every now and then somebody has wandered off and squeezed through the door . . . never to be seen again. It's been much safer to stay here, and there's plenty to do anyway.

In the time we've been here in the nursery we've really made some progress. It was all rather basic at first. Just four walls and a ceiling with a rooflight. Some embryonic furniture, bricks and other materials to play with. Gradually we've become more sophisticated. Our toys are really clever, and even practical. We can make more of what we have. And we can do trades and raids to get a little more, which is fun.

Yes, the nursery is a great place. It's just that it's a bit of a mess. And some of us have this nagging feeling that we may have completely missed the point. Or at best that there's more to it than we've realised.

The door is ajar. It was easy not to notice because of all the boxes and materials piled against it. But they've cleared a path through now and given the door a push. It's amazing what lies out there. To think we've been living in the middle of it all this time!

REDISCOVERY

Over the centuries humanity has experienced many great leaps forward. To be more accurate, a few have leapt forward, while most have resisted or ignored it, and some have gradually come on board later.

Explorers have taken us all over the planet and in the early days there were fears they would fall off the edge or be devoured by monsters. We have soared into space and plumbed the depths of the oceans. Our understanding has grown immeasurably, though not always smoothly. Galileo was considered a heretic for suggesting that the earth went round the sun – something Greek and Roman philosophers had realised centuries before. And the long-running Flat Earth Society had (and probably still has!) a loyal following.

Science has also made remarkable discoveries. And philosophy, from which science developed, strives to take us to deeper levels of understanding – the nature of existence, morality and meaning. Always there is resistance to let go of the old-established ways of thinking and doing things. Then gradually it becomes part of the bar-room talk. Each new discovery strikes us as remarkable, and extraordinary. Yet everything we discover was already there. Our learning is always rediscovery or, as Plato put it 2,000 years ago, a process of guided remembering.

So it is with abundance. It has always been there.

For thousands of years human society has looked forward to a Golden Age. The Greeks even felt that they experienced it, though largely in retrospect. Otherwise, we seem to feel it is an ideal to work towards. It's always just around the corner, over the hill. Our assumption is always that abundance is somewhere else, and we have to journey and break through to get there. We have to compromise, work hard, take more and more.

Now, as in so many of the old myths, we are coming to realise that the pot of gold does not have to be searched for in distant lands: it was at home under the bed all the time.

INTRODUCING ABUNDANCE

This book is an attempt to set the scene for a wholly new attitude and approach to money, wealth, the use of resources and abundance. A growing body of people has been moving towards this new reality for some time now. We will be summarising and acknowledging some of this work, while explaining how and where it falls short. Then we will look at what improvements are possible and at what deviations have crept in and, having been experienced, can now be released.

Chapter 1 points out how two fundamental streams of human existence have become polarised, how and why these polarities are being balanced now, and what benefits may be achieved by doing this.

Chapter 2 continues with an assessment of how money has come to be used as a demarcation line between two worlds. How we, as individuals, interface with money speaks volumes about the extent to which we are bridging the gap between old and new paradigms. At this point in the book the focus will be largely on the old, distorted attitudes.

The Author's Tale is recounted in Chapter 3 since the one thing that we can most usefully share is our own experience. Chapter 4 then completes the summary of how we have arrived at this point of transformation. This prepares the ground for the next five chapters, in which is set out what is involved in entering abundance, as opposed to merely prosperity.

Chapter 5 looks at resistance to change and helps you get out of your own way. And Chapter 6 provides a *discriminating* statement of the familiar, but hackneyed idea that we create our own reality. This idea has been grossly oversimplified and you will find it subjected here to more rigorous qualification than is usual. The result is a tool that works positively, rather than as an excuse or flagellum.

Chapter 7 introduces the Seven Level Model as it relates to the process of entering abundance. This model is the basis of most of the work The Breakthrough Centre is doing, integrating work and personal growth. Chapter 9 also uses this model as a framework for creating a practical action plan for yourself. Chapter 8 is about living in the abundant space between the old and the new. This is a subtle, often paradoxical place, free of comfortable but disempowering dogma, and requiring split-second timing and balance.

Much of my experience comes from self-employment – both enabling others and practical first-hand experience. Self-employment is a wonderful context in which to practise and experiment with abundance and trust. Chapter 10 looks at the issues involved in self-employment and the world of business generally.

The Afterword puts all this work into a planetary context, because when you work with abundance, you work with and for the planet. And what is best for you in the Age of Abundance is also what is best for the planet. You can then see your efforts extend beyond your own backyard and out into the planet. In this important sense this is a 'green' book. Abundance and planetary custodianship, like charity, begin at home.

This is where we are heading and now we need to return to looking at the present situation and why things have come to a head at this time.

THE NEW MILLENNIUM

As we move into a new millennium, most of the attitudes that have prevailed over the last one or two millennia are having to be reviewed. Birthdays and New Years are natural times of review, and rather more significant and considered than weekly or monthly reviews. Becoming a teenager, passing 21, arriving at the magical 40th year are all milestones in life's progress. The age of 100 rates a telegram from the Queen in Britain. So it is natural to reflect as one century passes into another, all the more so when the new century is also a new millennium.

Whenever we focus on anything, a new direction, our future, new priorities, we set something in motion. You have only to set your heart on a new mountain bike and suddenly the world is full of them. They were always there, it was just that your focus was not trained on them. Anything we focus on comes into sharper relief and impinges on our awareness. The more people who focus in a particular way and share their focus with others, the more this generates a collective focus. So when, at the end of a millennium, a great many people reflect on where we have arrived and look for a positive future, this creates a major shift in the collective consciousness. And this in turn attracts attention and draws others into focusing on it.

It is therefore entirely natural that the momentum for major change should be accelerating as 2001 looms larger.

There is no guarantee that change is any more urgent now than it was 20 or 60 years ago. In fact if humanity had recognised the seriousness of its impact on the planet (and humanity) 20 or 60 years ago, we might be looking at quite different issues now, but we would still be looking. Something clearly is not working now. But something was not working 20 and 60 years ago. The difference is that our *focus* is on it now, and our lack of focus before this has seriously aggravated the situation now.

A RAY OF HOPE

As the next millennium approaches, we can see that things are clearly falling apart. Perhaps things *always* seem to be falling apart to those living through them. Perhaps we should just shrug our shoulders and walk away. Or should we take the bull by the horns and say 'Enough and no more'. That is the view behind this book.

Without getting too depressed and allowing our negative attitudes to contribute to the prevailing doom and gloom, let us at least assess what is happening at the moment and acknowledge the different options and where they take us. Pretending nothing is wrong, sitting on our fears, repressing our feelings of anger, dismay or hopelessness is no solution. And neither is blaming others for the mess we are clearly in. We are responsible, even if the current situation has resulted from the actions of those in whom power is concentrated. We probably had more of an excuse 200 years ago when the madness of the industrial age began. Power was very much vested in the hands of a tiny oligarchy then. But alongside (rather than because of) the process of industrialisation has flowered a movement that encourages personal growth, freedom and individuation.

As a result we no longer have any excuses. The right to be self-determining has been hard won. One last shove might do it, especially as the old ways of thinking are so weak and destitute. The battle is being fought now on our terms. It is not like a war where might is right. Its weapons are not understood by the other side, and are not available to them. They are the weapons of personal freedom, positive consciousness and vulnerability and they are immune to power ploys and financial bribes. So we have the means to take over as the old system falls away.

Of course, 'the old system' is not that old. It is outmoded rather than old. Much of the 'new' thinking coming through now predates the industrial age and even the Christian era. What is new is our consciousness and awareness. The rest is as old as the hills.

WHAT WENT WRONG?

The oligarchy, initially with our self-preserving submission, but gradually with our self-serving connivance, focused on power, money and their accumulation, regardless of the consequences and impact on others.

Some of that impact has undeniably been beneficial. Our lives are more comfortable and convenient. We have opportunities to travel and communicate more widely. Our world has opened up and we are spared much of the pain and anguish of the past. I remember that each time I visit the dentist!

But what a heavy cost there has been. Much of the drudgery remains, just in a different form. Nature has been despoiled. Pollution is rife. Population is out of control; and while we cull everything else we don't seem prepared to curb ourselves. Travel and communication reveal to us the horror of starvation and deforestation that our greed and accumulation have created . . . if we care to look. Industrial development is out of control because we keep trying to catch our own tails. All over the world politicians, in our name, are losing the battle to overcome the problems caused by that narrow focus on power and growth.

Having encouraged acquisitiveness by their example and value systems, politicians now find themselves unable to deliver the dream or the promise. Their engine is running out of steam. It relied on increasing consumption, and growth for the sake of growth. But growth beyond a certain point is always at the expense of something else. And that certain point has been passed.

Growth has been achieved at the expense of other countries which were thoughtlessly stripped bare, and at the expense of various social groups throughout these last two millennia. It culminated in the naked greed of the industrial age, from the millionaires of the nineteenth century to the asset-strippers of the 1970s, and the yuppies of the 1980s, all taking their lead from the example of Imperial England's treatment of Africa, India, Ireland and elsewhere.

None of our potential leaders has been prepared to grasp the nettle and say, 'Money is not the priority. A new refrigerator is not the ultimate happiness. This is madness.' It is the nature of greed never to have enough. As more and more people have demanded fair shares over the last hundred years, the process has been one of trading up rather than meeting somewhere in the middle. The universal aim has been to have something approaching the lifestyle that only 3 per cent of the population used to have. To achieve this requires a staggering level of growth, and there has never been enough to satisfy the unrealistic demand created, nor will there ever be.

However prosperous the industrial age has made us, there never seems to be enough to satisfy people or politicians. We just don't seem to know when enough is enough, and so it goes on, with more and more of the planet being turned into rubbish we can do without. The appeal is insidious. Who hasn't, from time to time, hankered after a new car, slavishly followed the latest fashion, eaten and drunk to excess or coveted their neighbour's mansion? The difference is that some have learnt that material affluence does nothing for the soul or even for their sense of joy and fun: and a large percentage of society, including most of its leaders, do *not* seem to have learnt this.

TINKERING WITH THE MACHINERY

It was never achievable, but while there was growth, the pretence could be concealed. Now as growth grinds to a halt, and the recessions get longer, deeper and more frequent, the lie is revealed. And still the response of politicians is to argue about how the cake is to be shared and how a bigger cake can be 'cooked', while it is increasingly clear that the cake has passed its sell-by date and is beginning to deteriorate. Occasionally attempts have been made to redress the balance and redistribute the wealth through taxation. But this only creates conflict and demotivation – because in a society where money is the only good, taxing the 'successful' to subsidise the 'unsuccessful' is a nonsense; because if you get to keep less and less of what you are judged by, what was intended to motivate becomes a frustrating demotivator. Something much more radical and strategic is needed.

When Philip of Macedon was instructing the ancient world in the delights and misery of empire, Demosthenes likened the

Athenian reaction to that of a barbarian boxing. Wherever you hit him that's where his hands go. There was no strategy, just a knee-jerk reaction to each new onslaught. And the Athenians were no slouches at empire and undemocratic action themselves. Read Thucydides' *Melian Dialogue* for the gory details. England, America and Russia have many 'noble' antecedents, and their criticism, of Iran, Iraq, Israel, Argentina, Japan and Germany is as hypocritical as it is correct. They set the example, and little has changed since the Siege of Troy.

Not long after the Second World War, Eisenhower said, 'The people want peace. And one day the politicians are going to have to let them have it.' That time has come. And still the political parties maintain their exclusive coteries and keep on fighting wars, both actual and metaphorical, to keep us at each others' throats, slogging away to accumulate more and more.

In Britain and the USA, the political systems are so constructed that new ideas are excluded. In both of these countries, the leader only has the backing of around 25 per cent of the electorate, and the difference between the first and second parties is marginal in terms of votes. Yet, whether the winner by a nose is Democrat or Republican, Tory, Labour or Liberal, the winner claims an unchallengeable mandate and imposes legislation that discounts the views and opinions of 75 per cent of the population. Children are excluded altogether: the world they inherit is the creation of a minority and 75 per cent of them then find themselves excluded. The political encouragement to have a larger share has back-fired: we want our share of the vote, of power, of decision-making, as well as of the money used to bribe us into submission. What was acceptable in the days of Lloyd George cuts little ice now. Increasingly we demand to be heard, and frustration grows as the people become more aware and the politicians hide behind a political system that excludes them.

Sadly, when the system finally gives way, as it has already in the Commonwealth of Independent States (once the Soviet Union) and Eastern Europe, the floodgates are opened, and many of the new voices that are heard are even more strident and divisive than what they replace. The old demands and priorities persist but the structures have gone. There are new voices but not always new values. Money, power and growth are still seen as the only priorities. The focus is still on how the same old things can be differently distributed. Little changes and the only result is further tinkering with the machinery of an old, worn-out engine.

DISASTER SCENARIOS

There is a striking parallel here with Emperor Nero 'fiddling while Rome burns'. If your only reality is the cynical game of growth, it is impossible to see the other reality of planetary devastation. If your focus is on short-term gain and damping down the fires, you are blind to the long-term mathematics. You cannot see the effects of the measly 3 per cent annual growth in production that appeases the hungry mob you have created. You cannot see that 200 years from now, that means you will be producing and consuming in one day what now lasts a year. That means 365 times the devastation and counting. The old way cannot sustain itself. It is unsustainable. We are running out of resources, and running out of planet even faster. So we do not *have* 200 years. We have had them. We have had 200 years of that temporary aberration, the Industrial Age. Either *it* is over or *we* are over.

The disaster scenarios of the environmentalists (and even a few quite staid scientists) have almost penetrated the political consciousness. But they don't know what to do with it. They pay lip-service to the idea of 'saving the planet', but only when the people break ranks and look like breaching the defences of the electoral system. When that threat subsides they all revert to the old games, growth economics, electoral bribes, half-truths. In Britain the Labour party still behaves as if it is 1930. The Tories (Conservative is a meaningless term) still think it's 1830. While the Liberal Democrats have at least attempted to move the clock forward, they are barred from serious involvement by an electoral system designed to cope with the nineteenth-century reality of a two-party system. None of the parties' belief systems is relevant to the environmental scenario of 2030. The problem with disaster scenarios is that they are too appalling to contemplate. Moreover, the danger is that they become self-fulfilling prophecies. They are an essential foil to the politics of greed, but they still exist in that world of fear, scarcity and separation.

A NEW SPIRIT

Disaster scenarios may hold in check the worst excesses of the old ways. It will take something else to achieve the transformation that is needed. It requires a new impetus, putting energy into a positive option, rediscovering something we've forgotten or ignored during the last 200 or 2,000 years.

Peter Russell, in *The White Hole in Time – The Meaning of Now* (1992), advises that we get out of the materialistic trance, the hypnotic seduction of media images and let the hidden observer, our aware inner consciousness, take over.

Steve Gaskin is living proof that there is another way of approaching the situation. Having, in the 1960s, become the focus for thousands of San Franciscans looking for an alternative to the fear and spiritual degradation of American society, Steve set out with 50 busloads of people to find a place to start a new community. He says of this time, 'we became a virus in the American Freeway system!' Eventually, and probably to everyone's relief, they settled on a site in Tennessee, which is to this day simply called The Farm. He says, 'If you're not scared about the way the world is, you're simply not paying attention.' But he is not disempowered by this. He and his community on The Farm live by a belief in abundance and take their abundance out into the world, while politicians are still shuffling papers. He responds to disaster with practical action, love and education.

It is time to look at things differently and acknowledge our abundance.

Over the last 30 years we have experienced regular cycles of boom and bust, belt-tightening and expansion, recession and mindless growth. *Each* cycle offers us the opportunity to learn gratitude for all we are given, restrict our avarice, and invest in culture, education, self-development and future peace. Now, because prosperity has failed to teach us self-restraint and the adoption of a responsible set of values and priorities, we are being offered another way of coming to this realisation.

And this time it's permanent. Recession is a technical term used by politicians. It means that production of goods has not increased for six months or more. Yet it actually describes an ideal state in which there is no longer a senseless imperative to increase production. As animals we reach a certain size, pause and get smaller, before passing 'Go' and collecting a ticket to the next game. Why not economies? What says there has to be non-stop growth? Why do we need to concrete over more countryside to build more homes when there are still thousands of derelict buildings to be repaired or rebuilt? Population growth? Why? Isn't six billion people in the world enough? The truth is that growth is necessary to conceal and pay for the political and economic blunders of the past. We should be wise by now. We should have reached that quieter, more contemplative way of being that comes with years. And the good news from the 1990s is that that wisdom is more and more in evidence.

The old way clearly does not work. And a new spirit is coming through that clearly *is* working. This new spirit is more self-aware, more inclined to take personal responsibility, more concerned with personal inner growth than with monetary outer growth. It is less materialistic, less obsessed with the old definitions of success, less hostile and aggressive. And it is not nihilist or self-effacing. It is not into poverty consciousness, vows of abstinence, turning its back on the world and the hard-won comforts of modern living. It seeks and finds a correct balance between having and hoarding, power over and care for, giving and receiving, success and inadequacy. This is the subtle space of abundance which this book explores.

BREAKING THE ADDICTION

When viewed from the perspective of society's standards and social pressure to conform, the task that faces us can appear daunting. However, we have the encouragement of knowing that the gods of modern society are flawed.

Money as the primary measure of success does not work, at an individual level any more than at a collective, societal level. Psychologists and aware business people have had this information for years. Money is not a motivator, it is a potential demotivator. It stops people leaving a job, it does not motivate them to stay. Its only effect is to depress and demotivate those who do not have it or who have had it taken from them. Only days after a payrise, the warm glow wears off, and unless the circumstances of the work itself are rewarding, you have a disruptive, uncooperative team on your hands.

Yet the circumstances of people's lives often are less than fulfilling. And slowly increasing doses of money are injected to try and counteract this. It is not so much a reward for services as a compensation for boredom, a substitute for real satisfaction and fulfilment. So when the supply of the narcotic is cut off, as happens when growth stops in the economy, the symptoms it was repressing burst to the surface. As in natural medicine, the answer is not to keep on treating the symptoms, but to get beneath the surface and heal the cause. Once we can put money in its place, it may be that we have removed the major block to feeling abundant. Along the way we will need to deal with the resistance to let go of the addiction, and then we can be healthy.

The problem is concentration. A substance like coca is quite harmless naturally in the right circumstances. It is its concentrated form, cocaine, that is dangerous. Even morphine in small doses is useful, though there are natural medical regimes like acupuncture that are as effective without so much danger. So it is with money, as we shall see in the next chapter. In sensible quantities and with careful management it can be quite harmless and even useful. One just has to be sure who or what is in control.

Picasso, of all people, warned that we are possessed by our

possessions. Let us have money work for us and not allow it to run our lives, or overrun us. Let us be open to having our needs met, without denying ourselves the chance to come to terms with *real* life. Let us come into a new relationship with money where it is the servant of our search for meaning, not the master. Let us find and use wisely the abundance of the planet and not plunder it for fool's gold.

It is not money itself, but the *love of money* that is the root of all evil. There is nothing intrinsically wrong with money. It is one symbol of the abundance with which we are all endowed. Money, like any powerful drug, is only bad or dangerous when it is concentrated, accumulated and generally abused. But try telling that to the addict.

The addict craves another fix: death rather than life, deterioration rather than health. And we will defend our addictions 'to the death'. 'Even God drinks coffee!' says Carolyn Myss, whose intuitive diagnosis is as accurate as a brain scanner. 'I'm communing with the Tobacco Deva,' say I. Likewise when unlimited abundance is on offer, many still opt for the poor substitute: money. This love of money blocks the path to abundance, and keeps it hidden from us.

Abundance is therefore more accessible by those who place mere monetary success lower down their list of priorities – but not necessarily at the bottom of the list. The church mouse can miss out too, if in eschewing wealth and prosperity, it still fails to discover happiness.

There is a close correlation between happiness and abundance, and it will be important to keep this in mind and in heart throughout our exploration of abundance. Happiness has the power to generate the funds needed to sustain you and it. No amount of funds can generate happiness, unless it has found a place in your heart already.

FAITH AND FOOLISHNESS

Entering abundance does not necessarily involve ditching your entire belief system and means of subsistence straight away. Abundance is something you can allow gradually to replace whatever in your current approach does not serve you. In fact, ditching everything you have right now can be a way of denying abundance.

There was a man who had a firm belief that God would look after him. So, when the reservoir above his house burst and the waters began to submerge it, he turned away the boatmen who came by to rescue him, saying 'God will save me!' And when the waters rose and he was clinging to a chimney, he turned away the helicopter that offered him a rope to safety, saying 'God will save me'. And he drowned. And when he arrived in the other place, he took God to task. 'A fine friend you turned out to be. There was I trusting in your protection, and you let me drown.' To which God replied, 'What more could I have done? I sent you a boat. I sent you a helicopter. And you rejected me.' 'Oh,' said the man.

Abundance, like divine intervention, can take many forms. So your current income may be just as much abundance as locusts and wild honey. 'Baking bread', says David Spangler, the writer and educator on cultural transformation and spirituality, 'is just as much a manifestation as having it fall out of heaven.'

We just have to find a right balance, where money enhances and does not block the way forward. And we have to steer a careful course through the different forms taken by abundance and its opposite, acting out of distrust. Imagine yourself in a hot-air balloon. As the balloon fills, the bags of sand and stays keep you on the ground. Only when you are ready is it wise to cut the ropes. Otherwise you will be dragged off and will never get airborne. The bags of sand serve a similar purpose. Without them you may float away altogether and be lost: but with too many of them your progress and ascent will be slowed and limited.

Let's let go of the ballast. But let's take it gently!

IS THIS FOR YOU?

Whether you have 'failed' according to the old superficial criteria, or 'succeeded' and started to question the relevance of those criteria, this book is written for you. Even those who operate 'successfully' within the old criteria can find new dimensions to accelerate their progress and provide a structure for enhancing the second half of their lives. Those who are already on the path of abundance and coping 'successfully' with its demands and challenges will find insight and confirmation in what follows, together with increased clarity of the issues and how to handle them. And those who have tried to enter the Age of Abundance and found it difficult will also find reassurance and new, practical ways of breaking through.

Let us enter the Age of Abundance together.

> **There is never enough money or prosperity to create abundance.**

2

The World Makes Money Go Round

Money was meant to make things simpler. The mind boggles at what the camel economy was like if money was supposed to be less complicated!

A NEOLITHIC JOKE

The theory goes that money was invented because it was easier and expedited trade, much more convenient than trying to calculate what percentage of a camel was fair reward for a day's work. I can't see it myself. I would have thought it was much simpler to know when you had enough camels. When you couldn't move without tripping over one, I reckon you'd be pretty clear you had your quota! And when you had sheep's yoghurt coming out of your ears and people avoided you in the street because they too had your yoghurt coming out of *their* ears, it would be time for a celebratory sheep roast! This, I suppose, is where the marketing man was born, coming up with new uses for all those old sheep you had lying around!

I think it's much more likely that money was created as a tool for personal awareness by some early practitioner in consciousness expansion. It probably all started as a bit of a joke on a neolithic weekend workshop and became enshrined in the ritual of those times. The new consciousness is really so old. We've just remembered it, and the part money played in it.

We're realising that somewhere along the way – round about Egypt perhaps – the whole thing got totally out of perspective and the tributary became the river.

A joke turned sour

Over the years we have become obsessed with the stuff. It represents some sort of safety in what is seen as a dangerous, unsafe world. The more of the stuff you can pile up, the safer you will be. Tell that to anyone who was around in 1929 or any of the other times when the stock market has crashed. It happens with the same monotonous regularity as the fall of the autumn leaves these days, and what is the result? A feeling that you have to accumulate *even more* of it, because it might all crash again. Like all addictions, it feeds off itself. The last cigarette sets up the need for the next one. Last night's Mogadon ensures nothing so certain as tomorrow night's Mogadon. And no sooner has everyone settled down after the battle for their last pay rise than they are looking for the next one. There is never enough money to satisfy the desire for money, and resistance to getting off it is quite as fierce and painful as the resistance to getting off heroin. This explains why a lot of people are determined not to have anything to do with it, not to be contaminated by it, not to lose their souls to it.

The trouble is that unlike alcohol, tobacco, prescribed drugs and the ones we already recognise as deviant, money *is* also terribly useful! Your company is not going to go out of business because there is not enough tobacco going through it! The bank does not come to a grinding halt for lack of a new consignment of aspirin! But if there is no money coming in (or something so similar to money it might just as well be the jangly stuff itself), then you will judder to a halt, just as if your car has run out of petrol or oil. Now many would argue that alcohol and tobacco have a very similar role in their lives! It helps to oil the wheels, it keeps the old machinery chugging along! The essential difference is that while many people find they can handle Monday morning without a drink or a cigarette, nobody, so far as I know, has yet found a way of living on fresh air.

DOING WITHOUT MONEY

There have been various experiments with moneyless societies, which do have their good points. They encourage inter-trading within communities, and they spare their users interest charges. Some things you might think twice about paying £20 for are easier to buy when all you have to exchange is a couple of hours weeding a garden, which provides a pleasant break you wanted anyway. Where they seem to fall down is that one person doesn't always want the services that another person who wants their service can provide, and so we get into the recording of debits and credits, and people building up surpluses and accumulating overdrafts. Now if you have a whole gang of food producers in your so-called moneyless system, then maybe you get to take care of the basics by exchanging your services for food. But how long will it be before the chicken farmer has had so many massages he begins to feel like a punch-bag? How long before the shopkeeper has such a long line of credit for astrological services that she could, without too much difficulty, purchase one of the smaller planets herself?

WHAT'S IT FOR?

Such attempts at getting round the issue of money miss the point. Like anything we seek to evade and get round cleverly, it's going to find another way of sneaking up on us and tapping us on the shoulder. The fundamental issue around money is that our attitudes to money and our sense of self-esteem are inextricably linked. At both ends of the scale there are problems. Those who seek to accumulate piles of it are putting out a message that they doubt not only their value, but also their very existence, unless they can surround themselves with things that prove they exist and are valuable. At the other end of the scale, those who dislike the whole idea of money and are embarrassed by it are also making a statement about their own self-worth. Those who value themselves and have a positive attitude of their worth find that their needs – financial, physical, whatever – are always met. They have enough money and resources. Only those who are obsessed with money, either as something of overriding importance or as something to be resisted at all costs, have problems attracting enough of it.

Money has no importance in itself, only in terms of our reactions to it, what it means for us and the lessons we have to learn from it. What you may be sure is that if there is no profit in an enterprise, that is the end of the enterprise – unless, of course, it is a charity dependent on other people having enterprises that make profits and subsidise it. But, equally, if profit is the overriding concern of the enterprise it will be lifeless, pointless and ultimately soul-destroying. People who are concerned with making a profit need to answer the question, 'What is the profit *for*?' The answer to that question reveals the real motivation and reasoning behind the enterprise. The money one receives in an enterprise is simply the fuel or energy to drive the vision, and without it the vision stays in the garage.

The job of a lifetime

However we got into this mess with money, we certainly have a lot of work to do on it now! In workshops on holistic work the issues around money always generate the most lively debate. We want it! We fear it! We are suspicious of it! We go to enormous lengths to avoid dealing with it, and yet given the place it has assumed in society, we are kidding ourselves if we think we can have *any* sort of income without being clear about its place in our lives, how much of it we need and what to do with any surplus. Most of the resistance to receiving money arises from the abuses of those who have sought to accumulate too much of it. We don't have to be like them and, of course, the only reason this has a 'buzz' for us is because at some level we each know we are capable of that mill-owner tyranny.

A good living

A predominant attitude in Western society is that money is the only good. Accumulating money and the goodies it buys is all that matters. At the very least, money comes first and then things like relationships, family, environment might get a look-in . . . if there's time. The only criterion of success is money. Losing your money is the end of the world. The most important feature of any job is the price-tag on it. Greed is the creed.

At the other end of the spectrum, there are those who feel that money is evil and those who have it are evil, regardless of what they do with it. For any such person to have money is a fall from grace. They resist money coming to them, and are ashamed of it. This resistance to money is as obsessive as the endless pursuit of money. It *is* possible to be comfortably moneyless. This is one possible end result of having worked with money issues and come out clean the other side. But as long as you have 'stuff' around money and people with money, you have major work to do on self-esteem and self-respect. That's not a judgement. What else are you here for except to learn to love and value yourself?

The principal tool for learning this lesson is money. The schoolroom is the world of work. And that is what work is for. Work is a place we each create in order to grow. Primary relationships are the other schoolroom, and almost everything this book says about money is true for those relationships too.

This book is a search for the middle road, where money flows to meet our needs. It is the search for 'a good living'.

The honest truth

Money is no measure of abundance. It is more of a block to abundance. And it is, as a result, a marvellous measure of the task that faces us in adopting abundance. Along the way it provides us with a hilarious series of lessons, though we may not appreciate the humour at the time.

So far we have taken a broad sweep of the subject and looked at the overview, the big picture, the macroeconomic mess. There is nothing in this to suggest that a solution either to our monetary crisis or to our reluctance to embrace abundance will come from a political decision. Politicians are trapped in a situation largely of their own creation. The most honest politicians this century have been Václav Havel and Lech Walesa, who on appointment to supreme power announced that they could do nothing. They had merely presided over a shift to a new situation in which each individual could take responsibility for themselves. No longer could the electorate look to or blame politicians for the economy. It was all up to them. It might take generations to achieve it. All that was certain was that politicians, by definition, had no solutions and no panacea.

This might sound like a recipe for anarchy and selfishness – handing over to a dog-eat-dog jungle. Many would say this accurately describes the situation they inherited. The great difference is that the leaders were prepared to trust the people to be responsible, to take only what they needed and share what was available. And the truly great leaders set an example of this themselves. They do not over-indulge. They do not seek to accumulate power or wealth to themselves. They lay down the loosest of guidelines. And they trust that things will find their own level, if they do not interfere.

This style of government is a response to the growing trend for individuals to want to be in charge of their lives.

Money and its use as a measure of success has been one of the most subtle and pervasive control mechanisms of the outmoded systems that are falling away now. Yet, even as we seek to mature into more beneficent attitudes to resources and our right to them, old belief systems around money still cast their shadow. Before you can defeat an enemy, you must know your enemy.

GETTING PERSONAL

It is now time to look at *you*. What are the issues *you* have around money? What is *your* relationship with money? What is it for in *your* life? What does it represent to *you*? We are dealing here with the belief systems that run your life. Some may *seem* to be positive beliefs, but anything that is in control of you and stops you trusting or valuing yourself without external validation is not positive.

You could be entering risky territory. You may feel depressed at the end of it. And you might even feel there is no hope for you. This may not be very pleasant, and it is likely to give you as bad a picture of yourself as you could imagine. We are, after all, looking at the most negative aspects of you. If you come out of it feeling there is no hope, recognise that this is a belief system at work too! It can be countered like all the others, but only when you're clear what beliefs you have that need to be countered. It is worth doing. It is indeed essential to do because it will reveal what stands in your way. The good news is that you have positive beliefs that empower you too.

The process of this book is to build your justifiably positive beliefs and help you empower yourself through a belief in abundance. On the way, you need to face the shadow side and use its energy positively too. Recognise that, whatever the result of this self-evaluation, it is run by your belief systems. It is not the truth, cast in stone and irrevocable. Don't use it as yet another way to beat yourself up. That just reinforces the side of you that gives you a negative self-image. It is only one side of you that sees the negative perspective. There are other sides that take a wholly different view, and they will be encouraged to flower as you read through this book.

If you feel any anxiety about looking at these issues, at least ensure you have a friend on hand as you do it. You must be the judge of whether you need professional assistance or should undertake the assessment as part of your ongoing therapy.

If you wonder what all the fuss is about, recognise how insignificant your difficulties are compared with those of many others.

Self-assessment

This self-assessment takes the form of two series of statements and questions. Your task is to score yourself according to how much each issue worries you. There are no right or wrong answers and everyone will have a different cocktail that keeps them awake at night.

A very low score might contain one or two overwhelming

concerns that have far more impact than dozens of smaller worries and a higher score.

A high score might indicate that you are more closely in touch with the beliefs that give you difficulty, and are actually more likely to break through than a low scorer who is still repressing old beliefs and may even not be aware of them.

The object is not to trick you or catch you out. Nor is the aim to give you a reward or a stick. The intention is simply to give you information to work with, and perhaps some reassurance that if you score 10 on two issues, there are 98 other issues with which you don't have a major problem.

Some issues may appear to have little to do with money. They are included both because money is used as a substitute for many things, and because our real concern is not with money, but with abundance, which has very little to do with money in the end.

Scoring your worry quotient
In this first section, consider the extent to which you worry about each of the questions and statements listed. Then give yourself a score between 0 and 10.

As a guide to scoring:

 0 indicates this is not an issue for you at all
 1 indicates you are barely aware of it
 2 indicates you are aware but unconcerned
 3 indicates it gives you pause for thought
 4 indicates mild concern
 5 indicates concern
 6 indicates deep concern
 7 indicates anxiety
 8 indicates deep anxiety
 9 indicates panic
10 indicates something approaching paranoia

Belief systems are always on the move, so there are five score columns for you to use.

The *first* column represents your level of worry now. Write today's date in the box under **Now**.

The *second* column represents your memory of how much you worried about this 10 years ago. Write the year in the box under **Past**.

The *third* column is for you to indicate how much you believe you will worry about this in 10 years' time. Write the year in the box under **Future**.

The *fourth* column is for you to get objective feedback from someone who knows you well. Write this name in the box under **Other**.

Ignore the *fifth* column for now. (See page 209.)

In practice you might like to record the answers on a separate piece of paper, especially until you have obtained feedback from a friend.

SECTION 1.

Money worries

	Now	Past	Future	Other	
1. How am I going to pay the bills?					
2. Money just burns a hole in my pocket					
3. I never seem to have enough money					
4. I don't know how I'd cope without money					
5. Money runs my life					
6. We must keep up with the Joneses					
7. I wish we could afford a proper holiday					
8. If I have less money, I'm not as good as they are					
9. I'm hopeless with money					
10. We must maintain our standard of living					

	Now	Past	Future	Other	
11. If . . . (insert your ogre political party) get in, we'll be worse off					
12. I must be doing something wrong if the money's dried up					
13. Bankruptcy would be awful					
14. Running out of money is so inconvenient					
15. I didn't have enough on me. I could have died					
16. If you're so clever, why ain't you rich?					
17. I have to bring home the bacon					
18. I'm so busy working I never have time for me					
19. What if I lose my job?					
20. I must keep my nose clean and watch what I say					
21. If I could just get promoted, we'd be okay					
22. I must work harder. Then we'll have more money					
23. Work is going to kill me					
24. How can I call myself a success?					
25. Meeting people is terribly expensive					
26. Nobody will love me if I'm poor					

	Now	Past	Future	Other	
27. How can I keep a relationship without money?					
28. How can I contribute if I don't have money?					
29. I can't afford expensive presents					
30. What if I can't repay the favour?					
31. He/she won't believe I love him/her, unless I buy lots of presents and treats					
32. Without money I can't control this relationship					
33. I'd have nowhere to live if this relationship went wrong					
34. I couldn't survive financially without him/her					
35. If I can't pay my share, I'd rather be dead					
36. Imagine having to shop at Oxfam					
37. I couldn't bear to lose this house					
38. I don't think I'd be very nice if I had a lot of money					
39. What if we can't afford private education or school trips?					
40. It's either new shoes for the kids or a washing machine					
41. I can't pay as much pocket money as their friends get					

	Now	Past	Future	Other	
42. I must leave the kids enough to be comfortable when I die					
43. Without money, I'd be powerless					
44. I feel I'm a victim of circumstances					
45. If the stock market crashes, we're finished					
46. We could lose all this					
47. My worst nightmare is running out of money					
48. I wonder if I'll ever get out of debt					
49. I don't have much of a pension					
50. Will there be enough to bury me?					
Total: Section 1.					

Assessing your beliefs

The second list is common beliefs. To what extent do you subscribe to them? The scoring system is similar to that for Section 1. And again, as a guide:

0 indicates the *opposite* of this belief is true for you

1 indicates it is simply not true for you

2 indicates it is of no significance

3 indicates it has had a minor impact once or twice

4 indicates it occasionally pops up

5 indicates this belief is/was present for you

6 indicates it is significant

7 indicates a deeply-held belief

8 indicates you often tell other people about it

9 indicates you're always telling people it's the truth

10 indicates it is a major guiding principle in your life

SECTION 2.

Beliefs that block you

	Now	Past	Future	Other
1. Money makes the world go round				
2. Money is the only measure of success				
3. Real men bring home the bacon				
4. Might is right				
5. Money talks				
6. Where there's muck there's brass				
7. Money opens all doors				
8. You've never had it so good				
9. There's nothing like money in the bank				
10. Put your money in bricks and mortar				
11. Land will always be a good investment				
12. Nothing comes cheap				
13. Nothing's for free				
14. There's no such thing as a free lunch				

	Now	Past	Future	Other
15. Put your money where your mouth is				
16. Put up or shut up				
17. The chips are down				
18. You have to work hard for what you want				
19. You can't have too much of a good thing				
20. It's no fun without funds				
21. Diamonds are a girl's best friend				
22. Money is my friend				
23. Women shouldn't have to go out to work				
24. The principal aim of life is to retire				
25. A fool and his money are soon parted				
26. The golden rule of money: don't run out of it				
27. The rich get rich and the poor get children				
28. I want never gets				
29. Money's hard to come by				
30. There isn't enough				
31. There isn't enough to go round				
32. Money doesn't grow on trees				
33. Always save for a rainy day				

	Now	Past	Future	Other
34. Blessed are the poor				
35. Take care of the pennies: the pounds will take care of themselves				
36. You can have too much of a good thing				
37. Power corrupts				
38. No one is to be trusted				
39. You soon find out who your friends are				
40. Money can't buy me love				
41. The rich don't make it to heaven				
42. Rich people aren't wise				
43. When money flies in, love flies out				
44. Call no man happy until he be dead				
45. Don't be such a Scrooge				
46. Profit is a dirty word				
47. Love of money is the root of all evil				
48. Money is the root of all evil				
49. But money is terribly useful!				
50. In every well-governed state wealth is a sacred thing: in democracies wealth is the *only* sacred thing				
Total Section 2.				
Add Total Section 1.				
TOTAL WORRY QUOTIENT				

What do your scores tell you? That's the primary test. Is the level of worry and anxiety acceptable? How potent do the beliefs seem to be? And how would it be if the beliefs had less impact and the worry disintegrated?

There is no right or wrong score. Perhaps a total of 500 is too high, perhaps 300 is too high. Perhaps 800 is good because it forces you to do something about it and put off the evil day no longer. Perhaps a score of under 200 indicates you're not aware of the hold these beliefs and worries have on you. The scores are more useful when compared with each other, and particularly with how others see you. And any single statement that elicits a score over 5 justifies deeper scrutiny.

You probably noticed that the list of beliefs included some that suggest money is a good thing, some that suggest it is bad and some that suggest it's just difficult. All have an impact and create undue attention on money. As long as you're focused on money as being important or difficult, essential to have or essential to avoid, your capacity to enter abundance is limited. You can almost certainly add to the list even more beliefs that stand between you and abundance. This list is not exhaustive.

It is also possible to produce a list of positive beliefs that release the stranglehold of money. 'All my needs are met. All I need is abundantly supplied before I am even conscious of it. Consider the lilies of the field: they toil not neither do they reap: yet Solomon in all his glory was not arrayed like one of these.'

Given the harsh, materialistic focus of modern society and the collective pressure to conform, it is hardly surprising that we have these unhealthy beliefs about money and that as a result we worry about our financial state. But what good does it do? What does worry create except more things to worry about? In the entire history of mankind worry never created so much as one little red cent. Worry is the most monumental waste of time and energy we have invented. It invades our working life, taking the joy out of realising our talents and potential. It invades the home and all our relationships, turning bliss and acceptance into self-destructive anxiety. It spoils the loving connection we might have with parents, children and partners. It feeds the power-crazy Ego and distorts the ambitions of nationhood. And in all these ways it undermines our sense of trust and self-esteem. Why do we give it house-room? What could possibly justify the loss of all that? The right to worry and substitute love with money? We must be mad. Indeed we are mad. We should give worry its marching orders and not react by worshipping money as the solution to all these ills, when in fact our obsession with it is the root cause.

WHAT DOES MONEY REPRESENT TO YOU?

Does money represent security? Then it can haunt you with fears of it running out, losing your job, finding your pension is inadequate because of inflation. This is a poor substitute for the sense of security that comes from having embraced insecurity – feeling safe from inside rather than because of some unreliable Linus blanket.

Does it give you the power and capacity to make a difference in the world? Then, without it you are powerless. How much better to find your inner power and know that the example of your life makes a difference. Power that comes from money is power you can lose overnight. When you rely on money to be powerful, you have no real power at all. You have given all your power to money. You have given your life away.

Does it give you control of your own and others' lives? What arrogance to think you can run my life better than I can, when you can't even control your own destiny without external validation. Money gives you about as much control of your life as a cart on a Big Dipper.

Money most obviously represents wealth and prosperity. But all this is transitory and meaningless. Its accumulation is just another proof of fear and insecurity. What matters is what the wealth is *for*. You will be better advised to focus on *that*, on your personal vision, rather than merely on accumulating money.

Saving for a rainy day only guarantees one thing – lots of rainy days. The motivation is the fear that one day there will not be enough, one day I will be unable to work, one day I will want to retire and stop working. And that fear creates exactly what we fear. People only retire from work they never wanted to be doing in the first place. Why punish yourself for 40 years so you can be idle for 10? Why not find a nobler vision for yourself and pursue it with joy for a hundred years?

When you set money aside to fund a development of the vision you're working towards, this is slightly different. You might well create a fund for expansion or some other new experience your present life path leads you towards. Are you sure you're not deferring happiness though? Could you not change your life and start doing, in some small way, the thing you're saving up to do later? It is so sad that people put off until age 65 what they might have enjoyed when they were 20 or 30. If you love travelling or drinking ouzo in a taverna or bicycling in Beijing, find a way of integrating it in your life now. Get people to pay you for enjoying yourself. You will be amazed how customers present themselves when you are living your vision. Pension funds and life insurance are dreary if you subscribe to them out of fear. Look at them another way. A pension or insurance policy is a device for allowing thousands of people, including the government, to invest in the next stage of your dream. They are a place to put the surplus a beneficent Universe has provided, until you are ready to expand your vision and put this extra energy to work.

Does money represent success? Is it the primary goal and focus in your life, or just a means to an end, or a sign that you're on the right track? Do you want it for itself or as proof that you're a winner? Or do you know you're a winner, whatever your financial situation? It is all too easy to buy into the rampant materialism of the 1980s and believe that life is measured in smart cars, extravagant salaries and other symbols of success. If you're comparing yourself with others, you've probably succumbed to the clutches of Ego, which is obsessed with accumulation and in love with money.

Money is frequently used as a substitute for love and appreciation. When the presents and treats it buys are more important than the act of giving or the giver, when the reward for your endeavours is more important than the gift of the work itself, when what you share is more important than the act of sharing, money love has taken hold of you and you are reliant on something outside yourself to prove you have any worth.

Do you love money or do you hate it? Are you comfortable or uncomfortable with it? Either way it runs your life. Those who react against the excesses of the past 20, 200 or 2,000 years are in as much danger as those who relish it. Hatred and disdain for money are equally negative attitudes. Church mouse poverty consciousness is as much a neurotic statement of disbelief in the abundance of the Universe as the millionaire craving their next fix of cash.

Even a casual take-it or leave-it attitude may indicate unfinished work around money, though it is perhaps closest to a healthy relationship. It is no use pretending money is not an issue. It is so deeply engrained in our consciousness we have to come to terms with it. We have to work through our feelings of love, hate, rejection, deprivation, superiority, inferiority, insecurity, imprisonment, power, control, resistance, disdain, judgement and fear. Then we can find a comfortable, healthy relationship where we acknowledge our right to survive and grow, and share in abundance. We can stop substituting money for love, self-esteem and trust, and start working with it as a tool for self-empowerment and understanding.

MONEY HAS NO VALUE

Society has allowed money to assume a wholly disproportionate place in our lives. Yet money has no value in itself, only in the value we give it, and only in our reactions to it. If we react with fear, it has power over us and we lose ourselves to it. If we react to its activities with the attitude that it is a challenge to work with, a lesson to learn, an opportunity to love and respect ourselves in spite of all outward appearances, then we react with love and we grow in love.

Money, therefore, does not measure success or wealth or security or even self-esteem. *Our reaction to it* is the measure of how much self-esteem we have, how much we are prepared to trust in ourselves and in the abundance of the Universe. Money does not measure abundance, but there is a powerful interrelationship between them.

The attraction of money as a measure is that it is so easy. Life is so uncomplicated when the only consideration is money. 'He's rich; he must be good/bad.' 'I have more than you: I must be a harder worker/cleverer/better than you.' 'I have a big house: that proves I'm a success.' 'This job pays more than that: it's a better job.' But it's uncomplicated because it's superficial. And at the end of this life-game, or even sooner, there is no satisfaction.

Looking at what the money is for, what you spend it on, can tell you more about your priorities, so you go beneath the surface and start to find your truth. You might spend it on:

- food;
- your home;
- personal growth;
- education;
- children;
- health and massages;
- books and art;
- theatre;
- parties;
- presents;
- your own business;
- travel;
- charity.

Or it might go on drugs, status symbols, extravagances, war games and power ploys. Whatever it is, look at *why* you spend on those things, and you'll begin to discover your real priorities in life. Keep asking why and you get closer to the truth.

MID-LIFE CRISIS

These are the sorts of questions people ask themselves at times of growth. When they ask these questions at around 35 to 45 it's called their mid-life crisis. If they're in their 20s they are called naïve. Younger and they are called precocious. Older and it's their dotage. None of these names is appropriate. They are just the value judgements money and its followers use to keep you under control.

In life you either become aware of the conflict between the material, career path and an emerging spiritual imperative, or you die to yourself. Call it whatever you will, it's the metamorphosis from darkness into light. And it's happening to people earlier and earlier. Most children see it. It's common in teenagers and many find their way to it in their early 20s.

So where do we learn that money is all that matters? This, too, is common knowledge now. We all know that as parents we pass the ideas of our parents on to our children . . . with a commentary of our own added for good measure. Some of these parents and children become teachers, politicians, local worthies, churchwardens, police and all reinforce the messages of childhood. They comprise society and give us experience of what rich and poor, U and non-U, OK and not OK look like. It's then up to us to choose what is real for *us*.

Growing up is the process of differentiation between what is true and what is bunk! And this process never stops. This book would not be possible without all the preliminary clearing work others have done before. And there will be other books after it that take us further along the path to wisdom.

The particular step we're taking here is into greater self-esteem and trust, by replacing the chains of money with the freedom of abundance. We have started by questioning prevailing attitudes to wealth, prosperity, success and money. We have looked in particular at what issues you and others have around money, what it represents and what relationships with it are harmful. This speaks volumes about what supports and what blocks your progress.

It only hurts when you resist.

Money has no importance in itself, only in terms of our reactions to it.

3

The Author's Tale

ONCE upon a time, long ago and far, far away – or so it seems – I started saying 'You call this life?' and I started to question all the assumptions my simple, struggling life was based on. Perhaps there was more to life than a career and the gradual accumulation of zeros. If I track back to find out when I started asking that question, I can remember when I was about 29 starting to write a book which was called *Business as if People Mattered* and became very interested in the whole subject of motivation and the 'why?' behind the 'what?' Caring about other people and about whether they were happy at work seemed to be a very low priority, or at best the means to an end. If they are happy they will work harder. I remember at around that time giving a little speech at someone's leaving party and saying that Jill was leaving because it was no longer fun to work there and something else that was more fun was attracting her away, and saying 'If it's not fun where you're working, change it, because that's the only reason to be there'. My audience listened in stunned, shocked silence. What I was suggesting was totally beyond their comprehension – all of them.

MORE FUN THAN WORK

Round about then I coined the phrase 'more fun than work' to mean both that life could have more to it than just work and the money it generated, and that work was meant to be fun – more fun than just work. I was always attracted to theory Y as opposed to theory X, and yet it seemed – and still seems – that the way business is set up and works theory X, bigger sticks and bigger carrots, is still the order of the day and, maddeningly, what still seems to work best. As long as the objective is profit, growth and advancement at the expense of humanity, there is really only room for theory X. This is what I was questioning. Initially I believed that tinkering with the machinery, bringing in more theory Y, care and sensitivity for people, would do the trick. As time has gone by I have become clear that the whole ball game has to change. It is not enough just to tinker with the machinery, in business any more than in politics.

Another point at which this question about life came to the fore was when I read Eric Berne's splendid book, *Games People Play*. It was a major eye-opener, and I have never forgotten that the book that set me on a new path was a simple little book, written in simple language, about real people and their experience. It was not a deep, theoretical textbook, full of complicated terminology and incomprehensible sentence structure. In the last 10 years or so I have seen myself as the same sort of gateway, making it possible for people to take the first steps of transformation, and over the last 5 years I have increasingly been making myself available as support and guide further along the way. Often as a result, accountants have become healers, engineers have become trainers, and generally people have shifted from work that disempowers them to fun that makes money for them.

ANOTHER WORLD

Even before this, when I was just 18, between school and college, I received a major shock to my complacent, conservative, superficial system, in the shape of a lady called Susan. She represented a completely different world; a world I intuitively knew was the only real world, a world of honesty, authenticity, in tune with nature and contemptuous of a materialistic culture bent on its own self-destruction. She made me question the career path I was on and the assumptions I was making, and allowed the possibility of something of real meaning and incomparable beauty – and I resisted like hell!

Before that, it never really occurred to me to question the rules. Life was clearly about working hard, coming top, getting exams and scholarships, only doing things you could do well, having fun if there was time, being responsible and taking care of yourself. Appearances were everything, and the game was called 'Getting to the Top of the Heap'. It was a good game, and I was good at it, and something very fundamental was missing.

I didn't know then about sub-personalities and psychosynthesis, so it seemed pretty strange to feel that I was two people – one following a career path working my way up the 32 layers of management in Unilever, the other dimly aware that all this was superficial and meaningless, and totally missed the point. But what was the point? Since then I have found that almost everybody around the age of 25 to 35 asks questions like, 'What about me? When does it get to be my turn? Forget about what I do, my role, my status in the pecking order, value me for me', and those who don't face these questions then get to face even harder questions 10 years later during the mid-life crisis.

LEAVING THE FUR-LINED MOUSETRAP

As I later discovered, at age 29, 'the Saturn return', is a classic time to be asking these fundamental questions. It is a crucial turning point in most people's lives, the beginning of a major new phase, where you let go of the life path you were set on initially and choose for yourself. It is often the point where people leave home, let go contact with parents and, if they have married early, leave their relationships to start again. Not that the stars and planets decide anything for us; at most they set up possibilities, decision points and it is up to you what you do about them. Most people don't see the possibilities and press blindly on to the next lost opportunity.

I became more and more uncomfortable about working to a set of rules and a meaningless game plan and I started looking at the self-employment option. I was 31. I registered my business on 1 January 1979 and the very same day the company, for whom I still worked, promoted me to the position of director! I have since found that whenever people make major decisions about the direction of their lives they get major feedback. The directorship, which I had been waiting for for five years, seemed to be testing me. Was I serious about running my own business? Wouldn't I like to stay in the supposed security of a respectable job? I decided that 12 months as a director would add to my credibility in approaching marketing directors of other companies for project work. So I stayed on and resolved to use the next year or so to make more contacts. By February 1980 I had had enough and was ready to step off the cliff and go self-employed. I had decided to leave at the end of February and three days before that my position in the company became redundant! More feedback from the universe! And a useful boost to my finances over the early months of self-employment.

Letting go of the apparent security of a job can be a big wrench. In one large company they call it the 'fur-lined mousetrap'. Many of the inducements to toe the line can be very seductive and comfortable, but the bars of the cage are just as real.

DISCOVERING VISION

I worked for about 12 months as a marketing consultant. And then, in June 1981, I came in contact with a small company called URBED, which was in the early stages of pioneering training and development programmes for new small businesses, which has been the context for my work ever since.

In large companies it never seemed possible to work with people as people, whereas in a small business where I could work with the managing director or a sole trader who perhaps worked with a small network of associates, it was possible to work on what I find is the most important aspect of business – the development of personal vision and individual excellence. I discovered the value of working within a peer support group at URBED, which included at that time Ronnie Lessem, Tony Morrison and Nick Falk. Through working with them I realised that many of the ideas I had about work and life were not just my own mental aberrations. Many other people like them and respected writers like Abraham Maslow, the founder of humanistic psychology, were questioning the assumptions of the prevailing society. Through them I was also introduced to the Centre for Social Development in Forest Row and some of the practical applications of Gurdjieff, Ouspensky and Fromm. But probably most important of all was the contact with Kevin Kingsland, who had developed a practical and accessible model of human interaction called Spectral Theory, because it used the seven colours of the rainbow as a shorthand code. My own understanding and development of this model forms a large part of Chapters 7 and 9 of this book.

FINDING MY NICHE

For five years, from 1981 to 1986, a lot of my work centred around URBED and new business start-ups, together with further marketing consultancy work for other clients. It was a period of consolidation, firming up on my approach and acknowledging the contribution I could make. It seemed crazy to put so much energy into helping businesses start and not then provide ongoing support over the first difficult 5 or 10 years. So, from 1983, I started developing post-launch follow-up programmes, and badgered various people in positions of responsibility within the government to look at funding such programmes. When, in 1985, they finally conceded and set up a small budget to sponsor post-launch programmes I was more or less the only person in London who could respond.

My fascination with practical psychology and the integration of personal growth with work increased. This took a major step forward when I finally found my way to the Findhorn

Foundation on the Moray Firth in Scotland, and got rather more than I bargained for! I had gone there to see if I could run workshops for them, and instead discovered a perfect learning context for myself. Much of what follows represents my experience and the conclusions I drew about integrating the spiritual dimension into the practical realities of life during my time in Findhorn.

THE ROAD TO FINDHORN

I arrived in Findhorn by a fairly circuitous route. Most people who get there have similar tales. I read the American writer, Marilyn Ferguson's *Aquarian Conspiracy*, and tracked down its UK arm, the Business Network, which is closely linked with Findhorn. But the journey really started when I first questioned the cultural norm 20 years before. What brought it to a head were the events of early 1985. I had established myself, buying a house I could barely afford with a usurious mortgage, but 1985 looked promising. Within three weeks interest rates had shot up and I had lost my two main sources of income. I was quickly in a cleft stick. The bank manager became most interested, and when I joked that I might even have to sell my house, he replied, 'I think that's a very good idea!' He *wasn't* joking. My heart sank. It wasn't just a house, it was ME being sold down the river. I realised I had more than money invested in that house. It represented my whole sense of self, proof that I was successful, a winner. My self-esteem and self-respect was wholly dependent on having my own front door, a garden and eight rooms in which to roll around on my own. I was in shock. I blamed everyone and everything. Feverishly, I looked first for good reasons, then explanations, finally just anything better than lame excuses for selling up.

The sale was slow and difficult . . . giving me time to get the message and wriggle on the hook. I was not to be allowed to get out of this without a fight, or without experiencing the humiliation it involved for me.

Once I had brought myself to admit publicly that I had been

stupid and was looking forward to living in a much more sensible, smaller flat, the house was sold and I found I had lived in it free for two years.

At roughly the same time I let go yet another in a long series of relationships in which I had sought to bolster my wounded pride and lack of esteem. My only remaining personality substitute was a red XR2 (and that too went during one of the annual Breakthrough Centre crises later).

I had let go of the things that appeared to confirm my sense of self, which actually *denied* that sense of self. So it was in a time of awakening that I arrived in Findhorn. And the angel I drew at the end of my first week? Abundance!

Catalysation

Findhorn (the Foundation, not the nearby village) is the most amazing place. It is probably the safest place on earth for you to become more of yourself. There is no dogma, no religion, no insistence on accepting a particular approach or moving at a particular pace. You learn and grow at your own speed; you take responsibility for your own experience. Nobody pushes you, nobody judges you and often, maddeningly, nobody spells out what the message really is − you find that out for yourself. And everybody supports your process in their own way (which may include ignoring you and challenging you, but is rarely harsh or unloving). Most people find their first week at Findhorn, whether on an experience week or a conference, is a transformation, which produces a profound catalysation and a turning point in their lives. Most people resolve to stay longer, or return later and regularly. I have been returning for seven years, for anything from a week or two to several months. If you are serious about stepping into your potential and being who you really are, I highly recommend it.

JUMPING THE TRACKS

Over the last few years I have set aside more and more priority time for personal growth and, as a result, my life is richer in every sense and personal growth has become the primary element in what I communicate in my trainings, counselling sessions and written work. There are literally millions of people in Britain, and as many in dozens of other countries around the world, who are following a similar pattern with their lives, starting on one particular set of railway tracks; becoming aware of other railway tracks and at some stage jumping the points and getting on to another track and from there into virgin territory where they create their own tracks day by day, hour by hour. I am only aware of one other book that describes the process of moving from superficial career to authentic inner-directed life within the context of work and the commercial environment, and that is Jonathan Clark's *The Barefoot Accountant*. There are plenty of books describing people's spiritual journeys, but how they integrated this with their daily working life and financial survival is largely ignored. To me it is important that people can feel that they can set out on this journey, the ultimate journey of discovery – the discovery of self – without having to become monks and nuns.

So I see my life now, not just as a series of lessons for myself, but also as a model or an example for others, that it is possible to be yourself and be real, and do what you enjoy rather than just enjoying what you do, and for that to work in pure commercial terms.

BREAKTHROUGH

In launching The Breakthrough Centre there have been countless invaluable lessons to learn about trust, letting go, commitment, manifestation, clear intention and right attitude, and many of them have been not without pain. I have no doubt you will see similarities with your own experience and find that many of my lessons speak to you as well, because trainers and therapists generally attract to them people who are dealing with issues that they, the trainers, have recently had to face themselves. That, for me, is the primary role of trainers and therapists, to share their growth and experience with others who are going through the same experience themselves. As you read this chapter I encourage you to compare it with your own experience of taking or considering major steps. You may well find that circumstances you had seen as negative can be reframed into something more positive.

Taking the plunge

The first lesson for me in launching The Breakthrough Centre was that a good idea often takes the wrong form initially. I was convinced that I should create a centre in Scotland first and work in the enlightened atmosphere of the Findhorn Foundation. I felt I could add a useful dimension to this centre for personal growth. I worked towards this for two years and arranged to hand over all my London business to other people in return for regular income when I visited London thereafter. Then I found that when it came to the crunch and I arrived in Findhorn in July 1987 ready to take the final steps towards becoming an independent member there, there was no real opening for what I could offer! In fact, within 24 hours of my arrival I had twisted both ankles – a sure sign of the need to change direction!

So then I started looking at gathering together a group of people for a collaborative venture in London, and again found that all the interest disappeared as soon as financial commitment was mentioned!

Colliding with destiny

The clear feedback was 'Do it yourself and do it in London'. I spent the best part of six months at Findhorn in 1987 and, at the end of my stay, was no clearer than at the beginning what I should be doing, but as I drove back from Scotland at the end of January 1988 it all came clear. Nodding off on the motorway and colliding with the central reservation helped! I quite literally woke up and all the thinking of the past two and a half years gelled in the space of five days. What emerged was the concept of my own training centre with space to hire, an information networking service, and an integrated programme of support for people taking charge of their lives through self-employment and other personal growth routes. New ideas, I realised, need a generous incubation period, during which there is plenty of 'active being', thought and the making of connections. Then, once the time is right, the conversion to a workable principle is fast. I had to reach the point of believing I could do it without dependence on others for credibility. So often the only person I have to convince is myself!

Energy follows form

Once the idea takes roughly the right form, and all the alternatives and soft options motivated by lack of self-belief and self-esteem have been given consideration and rejected, progress is fast. Energy follows form. The potential or energy is always there, we just have to find the right form or shape or channel for it to flow through and then step into it. Every single ingredient of the steam engine, for instance, was technologically available at the time of Julius Caesar, but it took 1,800 years for Watt to create the right combination for that energy to be harnessed. In my case the energy to be harnessed was the premises; I had known of their existence and availability for 12 months and, because I was looking first at Scotland and then at bigger schemes, had written them off – they were too expensive. And so they just sat there, prime, freehold office premises – at the time a virtually unobtainable asset, waiting for 12 months for me to realise I needed them. I viewed the premises on 2 February, five days after leaving Findhorn, and paid my £250 deposit to hold them for four weeks. I had 10 per cent of the money I needed to buy and equip them properly. Sixteen weeks later, having raised £122,000 and completed the building works, we opened. This is where the lessons about trust came in!

£86,000 please!

My first efforts to raise the money (through a specialist fundraiser) failed dismally. We were turned down three times.

The benefit was that I learnt what the proposal needed to say and what had to be done. The plan was not fully formed and something was blocking progress. Stepping back a little I realised that I needed to start the marketing process of identifying customers. Immediately funds started to flow in. I had avoided the obvious step of talking to my own bank. I phoned them on Thursday and said, 'I'm in a bit of a hole – I need £86,000 by Monday to secure a freehold property. Can you help?' We talked for a minute or two and the bank manager said, 'This is the sort of proposition we ought to be looking at, but I think we ought to see you!' I went to see him on Monday and he said, 'I can't get you the money today, but would Friday do?'

When things work out, it's always so easy. So I proceeded with the purchase, but then the funds stopped flowing in again, and it looked as though the project would fall through. Stepping back again I realised I had *said* I would do the marketing, but had not actually done it. As I implemented the marketing plan energy flowed again and the next bit of funding arrived.

The Angel of Trust

The same process of stepping back did not work for the last £13,000 of funding, but, looking back, I could see this arrived at the 11th hour and realised that this meant repayments started later, so the Universe was applying good financial management criteria! It also gave us rather less than we asked for on all fronts, so we ran all year on £11,000 less than I calculated I needed. Shortage of funds concentrates the mind wonderfully, while too much, too soon can breed complacency. When The Breakthrough Centre opened on 24 May 1988, the Angel of Trust was drawn from a pack of Angel Cards to overlight the Centre and it has been about trust ever since.

Putting out

For instance, I remember in August 1988 realising we were £1,500 short, so I 'put out for it'. Within an hour two phone calls (one in, and one out) provided nearly £1,600 and, sure enough, we needed that extra £100 too. Round about the same time, I needed help around the Centre, and again 'put out for it'. Within 48 hours the two people I needed walked into the Centre, and Fiona is still here taking a more and more active part in the development of the Centre and in my own personal life and development. Yes, I had put out for that too, and not realised I was looking for a total of two people, not three.

Creative worry

What more evidence could one ask for that one was on the right track? But I wasn't convinced! I had to make life difficult, because 'You only get what you want by hard work!' So every month I panicked about money – this month's money, next month's money, next year's money – it didn't matter, as long as I could worry about it! I learnt a lot about how productive panic is. It produced stress, paranoia and an expanding growth rate of things to panic about. With that one tool, worry, I dematerialised a major client and froze my shoulder for six months.

LETTING THE ENERGY FLOW

Our first birthday party went a long way to shifting the worry, as I realised how much love we were receiving, but what really cracked it was a commitment finally made in early June. I had been planning a holiday 'if I had time or money' and I was getting neither. When Fiona returned from a visit to Findhorn she announced we were both going back in August. I readily agreed and expressed my commitment to the idea she should be at the Centre on a much more regular basis because of all the work that was bubbling under. Within a day or two calls started flooding into the Centre. We were more stretched financially than we had ever been and the bank manager was reminding me that *we* were meant to bank with *them*, but the panic was gone, so the energy of money could flow. The lessons I learned through this were as follows.

1. Worry blocks energy (i.e. money). Worry indicates distrust in abundance. Stop worrying and abundance can flow.

2. Deciding to do something is not commitment. Booking the ticket is: only then does the Universe know you are serious and send you the funds.

3. When you have done O level trust you move on to A level. (We're now doing the Ph.D.)

4. Whenever we start thinking too big we get reminded to start dealing with the here and now. 'Think big, start small.'

5. When you are open to receive, listening to the feedback, clear and committed without being attached to the result, all your needs are met.

The bracing winds of change

We continued learning and developing through 1989 and, as 1990 started, I must say I was looking forward to a more relaxed year without too many financial anxieties. My guardian angel had other ideas and clearly reckoned it was time for us to leave the cosy nest of subsidy and spread our wings on the bracing winds of change. In March 1990 as a result of a dramatic U-turn in government policy, we found ourselves looking at a shortfall of around £30,000 of income for the year at very short notice. We were getting better at seeing the lessons in our experience, so after the initial shock and anger, we looked back at the plan for the year to see what new door might be opening as this old door seemed to be closing.

We had been attracting a steady flow of people to the Breakthrough Club and our workshops for two years. So this was where we looked to make up the shortfall from other sources, not least because it looked as though there would be very little other small-business development training available following the government's cutbacks.

Our aim became clear − to expand the Breakthrough Club's membership from 35 to 150 by the end of July. I frequently remind people on workshops that you have to make it clear to your customers and contacts that you are actually looking for more customers! Otherwise they assume you're too busy or would be insulted or something! So . . . we put out clearly for more customers.

Difficulties at the beginning

To help us achieve this, we asked ourselves what we were offering and to whom.

We called in a creativity consultant we respect, and then questioned a dozen people who knew us quite well to establish the following:

- How do we serve our customers?
- What do we actually provide?
- What do they see as our essence?
- What is our market?

We collated all the answers and used them as the basis for a brainstorming session. This brought a lot of much-needed clarity.

An oasis of peace

These were the main ideas that emerged. They represented for us a significant step away from compromise, towards being who we really are.

The Breakthrough Centre is a Business Centre with a heart, a Business Centre plus. It feels like a haven, an oasis of peace, a sanctuary in a crazy, crowded city. Above all, it provides space, support, practical help and success. We pull back the curtains, so you can see out of the window. We take the lid off. We open up your head and your heart. We create a space where you can learn and face unpalatable truths without feeling threatened or diminished. And all because of the space we operate from, The Breakthrough Centre.

These were key words with a lot of magic around them, and depths and connotations of which we were quite unaware before.

The essential message that emerged was 'YOU CAN': a fundamental shift is possible.

Work is the context for personal growth

Our 'target group' we clarified consisted of people who, to a greater or lesser extent, were working *for* themselves and working *on* themselves. These were business people looking for a deeper personal dimension; people whose antennae were up for business/personal/'spiritual' support; people 'on the path' looking to bring this into their work; people looking for 'something more', often unconsciously attracted without necessarily being very aware at first; those with a more alive sense of community (local and global). And also many, many self-employed people looking for straightforward business consultancy. In short we were targeting people who see business training and/or personal/self-development as an integral, priority aspect of their business. The Breakthrough Centre, we decided, was the only place that combined self-development with self-employment and business growth.

Since then we have moved on even more determinedly, to propose that work is the ultimate personal growth workshop.

Attracting abundance

We learnt a lot from the study about how best to attract 100 new Club members and, by the end of July, we had not 150 members, but the Club had grown to 70. (You can decide *what*, the Universe has the final word on *when*!)

We also focused on 'green, ethical, holistic, creative, artistic, spiritually-aligned businesses' and found that this *narrower* focus attracted *more* people to us, including many who would not normally describe themselves in this way, but found our approach made a lot of sense to them.

Releasing attachment

While we were implementing this rescue plan, we won a large contract from the Training Agency. This, together with other contracts that were resurrected at the same time made up the £30,000 shortfall from the previous contract with some to spare! This was, for me, a beautiful example of how letting go and releasing attachment results in getting what one wanted, but in a better, different form. If we had pushed and shoved and dumped our resentment all over the place I am certain we would not have been taken care of in this way, but by letting go our attachment to a particular solution, a better solution emerged. We expressed our anger, let it go, and the answer dropped into our laps. So, not only did we double the Club membership and establish a really firm base for its further growth, we also acquired new sponsorship to run programmes we had wanted to run for two years.

The news of the new contract came an hour before I set off to join 20 other people running Centres for a weekend gathering at Runnings Park. That group expressed a strong need for business training and support, and I was able to offer the possibility of free, sponsored events.

By being more real to ourselves, doing what we felt was right rather than constraining ourselves within a narrow perception of what we thought we had to do, the business worked much better.

We are, of course, not alone in this experience. Many friends report that when they decide to go self-employed, they suddenly start getting offers of *very* high-paid jobs (which they have usually been seeking for months before unsuccessfully). The explanation is simple – their energy is good because they're focused on being real. What you most need often comes in sideways, out of the corner of your eye, when you remove your attention and look the other way.

A striking example of how releasing this can be came one afternoon when Fiona decided what she most needed was to be quiet and relax with a good book. She would answer the phone and that would be that. The phone rang six or seven times that afternoon – resulting in £3,000 worth of new business, and further proof that being detached, relaxed and open can be very profitable.

REAL OR SUPERFICIAL?

This story demonstrates the importance of working with the spirit of the times, attuning to self and environment, and doing what is necessary. Holistic work is full of serendipity, coincidence, luck and challenges to the Self. It starts with Self and takes care of Self, whereas conventional work tends to start with superficiality and Ego and that is also where it ends. Both approaches work, but in different ways to different ends. One is fulfilling in itself in its process; one is obsessed with results and is rarely satisfying. You choose!

The role of relationship

Up to 1988, when I opened The Breakthrough Centre, most of my personal development work happened in personal relationships. I was dependent on having a good-looking relationship to prove my acceptability. The only way I could love myself was to be loved by somebody else – external validation. This gave me 25 years of alternately hurting and being hurt in relationships. There were occasional exceptions, that endorsed an undistorted sense of self, and I am just beginning to understand them now. As I think is clear from my story, Breakthrough has been the 'relationship' that involved no hurt, attracted the commitment that was usually lacking in personal relationships (on one side or the other) and created the space in which I could at least value myself, from the inside out. And it has this effect on hundreds of people who come through it too.

Having found this space of self-improvement, relationship has entered a new chapter. Carl Rogers says there is only relationship where there is mutual concern for each other's and one's own growth. This means a relationship must be able to cope with the shadowy side – to encourage it to be expressed, acknowledged and released. As long as we both grow, and provide support and challenge in that process, there is relationship. So Fiona 'calls me' when I get into old patterns of worry, misery, self-deprecation and self-congratulation, and facilitates the painful process of growth through existential angst and re-awakening feelings. I hope and believe I do a similar job for her.

Kid's stuff

My daughter Lorna, now 15, has also been involved with the development of the Centre, and our relationship has taken off as she has also embraced her own growth. Using the Centre as a base she has tried a number of formats for creating a safe space in which children handling the transition to adulthood can talk about things that concern them – with each other, rather than with adults who, however well-meaning, are too far removed from the problem to empathise. She ran her first workshop when she was 12 and appeared on Channel 4 television a year later. GCSE and the endless examinations school children are now suffocated by, virtually every day of the school term, have temporarily occluded this. But the need for children and teenagers to receive a *real* education, as well as being stuffed with information of often very dubious usefulness, is on the ascendant. I can see Lorna and the Centre returning to this theme before long.

Critical times

And so it is with much that happened during the heady days of 1989 and 1990. We started working with Russian entre-preneurs at the end of 1990, then in Ireland and at Cortijo Romero, the holistic holiday centre in the mountains of southern Spain in 1991. All this indicates where we may be heading. And it is not quite time for it yet. We receive hints of our future, and are then called to heel. The Russian connection falters: the first event in Spain is marred by the Gulf Crisis. And all this, of course, further tests whether such developments are awakening the self-important Ego monster.

All the time we are learning to be clear what we intend, and open to whatever is needed. The year of 1991, for instance, was brilliant for us up to August. I'd put out an 'impossible' intention and we were within 2 per cent of it on all measures. Then another crisis struck, and yet again it was changes in government policy that created it. Crisis always has something to tell you. And what these annual crises with government funding told us was 'You're doing something worth while. The Universe is supporting it with the funds you need. But you are *not* to depend on those funds. If you get complacent and stop moving into making your unique contribution, we'll pull the plug on you.'

Crisis forced us to re-evaluate. I seriously considered closing the Centre, assuming that although it was great fun I must have taken a wrong turn somewhere. Part of me was very positively practising saying 'I am not attached to the success of this place' and another resentful old part of me was playing second degree – 'Now look what you made me do!' I decided simultaneously that we were going to put everything into The Breakthrough Club . . . or bust. And I also decided it was time we looked for new partners/associates/sponsors to fill up the space vacated by the government's gradual withdrawal from support for small businesses.

What happened? We started attracting more, real, paying clients: the Club grew to 100 in four months; we have at least five extremely exciting possibilities for new associations; Greece and Scotland have been added to my list of venues for 1992/3; and we won back £9,000 of the government funding we lost. We still carry the overdraft the *last* crisis created, but this too teaches us volumes about how debt is also a form of abundance.

A leap of faith

Life has become a series of huge leaps of faith. Each time the tests get bigger – more to let go, more to risk, more to put out for, more to trust and more abundance as our needs grow and we respond to feedback.

The isolated 'I' that started this story, looking for a 'we' to validate it, has become an inter-connected 'we' that includes a self-dependent 'I'. This has happened, *as it will for all who undertake the journey*, through seeing work in a different way. For me it was first a living; then I saw it as fun. Then it became a context for personal growth, and next it is to be a healing process that ripples out around the planet.

Worry blocks energy.

4

Beyond Prosperity Consciousness

MY own experience, as outlined in Chapter 3, strongly suggests to me that there is an alternative to the disempowering, hard slog, rat-race of the acquisitive society.

It *is* possible to have fun, find fulfilment and enjoy a wealth of experience and even resources without being plagued by the demands and pressures imposed on us by the tyranny of money.

This may sound similar to the idea of prosperity consciousness which says that if you focus your consciousness on prosperity (positive thinking), rather than poverty (negative thinking), all your needs are met. However, I am reluctant to line up with prosperity consciousness and its adherents. I'm clear that the idea has its good points, but I'm equally clear that it has been misrepresented and hijacked by people who still subscribe to the outmoded idea that accumulation of money is the primary objective of life. And that is dangerous, destructive bunkum.

To release yourself from the dead hand of this philosophy, it is necessary for us to retrace our steps, rediscover the foundations of prosperity consciousness and distinguish between its positive potential and the wrongheadedness it contained. Sadly the wrongheadedness is largely what has been adopted by today's followers of prosperity consciousness.

The concept of prosperity consciousness is a child of the Industrial Age. It probably dates back to 1937 when, after years of research and interviews with the richest people of his time, men like Andrew Carnegie and Henry Ford, Napoleon Hill published a book called *Think and Grow Rich*. He was looking for a common thread, a set of principles, practices and behaviours that would distinguish the most financially successful from the rest. I believe that he found that distinguishing factor, and that it was lost when his ideas were misappropriated by those who still subscribe to the outmoded idea that money is all that matters.

Hill found that his group of wealthy men exhibited an exceptional degree of clarity of purpose, that their minds were sharply focused on the object of their desire, that they shut out anything that undermined this objective and constantly reinforced the positive. There is nothing too surprising in this, though as we shall see some of it is flawed.

His more surprising discovery was that the exceptionally wealthy also talked about having faith in 'the Infinite', creating a quiet place of meditation, co-creating with others for the good of all, transmuting sexual energy into a spiritual creative force and drawing on the guardian angel of creative imagination. Thought was creative, and thought had a strongly spiritual element. There was an ethical, spiritual component in effective wealth creation.

Think and Grow Rich was a name well chosen to attract readership, given the prevailing obsession with money and the fear of insecurity surrounding its loss in the uncertain years between the 1929 crash and the Second World War. The book could have been a stepping stone out of the old, distorted industrial ways into a more aware, caring approach to wealth creation and distribution. It made clear that there was more to getting rich than just sharp focus, and that sharp practice didn't even come into the picture. Real success involved spiritual aliveness. Look at what he actually said.

A SUMMARY OF
THINK AND GROW RICH

1. *Desire*

- Fix in your mind exactly what you want – in precise money terms.
- Determine what you will give in return – be a go-giver, not a go-getter.
- Set a date when you will possess the money you desire.
- Write it down, sign it and repeat it aloud first and last thing every day.
- This is your ambition, your burning desire, your passionate purpose.
- See, feel and believe yourself already in possession of the money.

2. *Faith*

- Have faith in yourself and in the Infinite, to create positive thoughts and your good 'luck'.
- Know that your dominant thoughts manifest concretely, eventually.
- Concentrate on positive thought 30 minutes every day and on self-belief 10 minutes a day.

3. *Autosuggestion*

- Create a quiet place to focus on your desire with total faith every day.
- Keep a written copy of your statement of desire in a place where you keep seeing it.

4. *Specialised Knowledge*

- Go to those who can give you short cuts to specialist information.

5. Imagination

- Use synthetic memory imagination to organise things.
- Use creative imagination to tap into new ideas, inspirations, hunches.

6. Organised Planning

- Create a definite plan for acquiring what you desire, and add this to the statement of desire.
- And begin NOW, ready or not.
- Develop yourself as a leader with courage, self-control, sense of justice, decisiveness, a pleasing personality, sympathy, understanding, mastery of detail, willpower to assume responsibility, co-operation and a readiness to do more than you're paid to do.

7. Decision

- Decide to do it . . . develop your willpower.

8. Persistence

- . . . And don't stop till you get it. Keep saying YES when everything else points towards NO.

9. Power of the Master Mind

- Enter into a friendly alliance with one or more people you need to create and carry through your plans, and be clear what you offer them in return for their co-operation.
- Select life and business partners carefully, and retain self-reliance.
- Meet with your Master Mind group twice weekly or more often until the plan is perfected.
- Maintain perfect harmony with every member of the Master Mind group.
- Recognise that a group of brains creates a third force that is spiritual in nature.

10. Sex Transmutation

- Tune into the irresistible energy of sex, love and romance, especially available between the ages of 40 and 60.
- Transmute biological sexual desire into spiritual creative force and enthusiasm.
- Recognise that personal magnetism and charisma is simply well-directed sex energy.
- Experience the spiritual quality of love which connects you with the Infinite intelligence.
- Do only what benefits all, serving others.

11. Subconscious Mind

- Feed your subconscious with positive emotions – desire, faith, love, sex, enthusiasm, romance, hope.
- Exclude negative emotions – fear, jealousy, hatred, revenge, greed, superstition, anger.

12. The Brain

- Put your brain in gear, your subconscious sending out positive thoughts, your creative imagination receiving that thought energy and autosuggestion broadcasting to the world.

13. Sixth Sense

- Creative imagination is a guardian angel that is available through meditation and inner development.
- Select your cabinet of 'invisible counsellors', draw on their strengths and seek their help in solving difficult problems and responding to opportunities.
- Overcome indecision, doubt and fear ... the six ghosts of fear – poverty, criticism, ill-health, lost love, old age, death – and susceptibility to negative influence.

You create your own reality, because you control your thoughts, which always concretise.

Nowhere to hide

This distillation of Napoleon Hill's thesis can serve us well if we ignore the obsessive focus on money and the repression of 'negative emotions' and fear. Fear and negative emotions only have power over us if we run away from them and try to pretend they don't exist. Saying YES to life is very commendable: refusing to look at the parts that say NO is self-defeating. Affirmations are all well and good, but if they are used to shout down heckling belief systems, their effectiveness is very short term. The illness that is not treated at its root cause can fester into a cancer. We have to face it. This, too, is part of life's rich tapestry.

Our historical attitude to money could have developed from this point in a more ethical direction, with less emphasis on accumulation and more on connecting with our inner spiritual selves as a way of moving forward. This was Hill's great discovery. The spiritual element added something to industrial life, which not only made more money, it made more sense. It had the potential to restore balance to a world that was dangerously out of equilibrium, and bring the sacred back into our lives. Instead, the ideas of Napoleon Hill and his disciples were distorted to justify materialism and give it an ethical, holy quality it does not deserve. We took a step backward, selecting only what we wanted to hear, instead of a step forward, building on the spiritual, and removing the main flaw in Hill's book, the suppression of what was seen as negative.

Latter day prophets of prosperity

Napoleon Hill's approach was more balanced than the prevailing attitude of his time. He was presenting a better way of working with a bad old system, a way that the richest men of the time had proved worked best. But in developments since his book was written, the ethical stand and the connection with the Infinite which made it work best have been lost. The latter-day prophets of prosperity are dismissive of the value of anything except money and hopelessly attached to it to prove their worth. They have completely missed the point that the way to wealth creation is spiritual, and instead made a virtue of the immense effort and hard work that are necessary if one tries to get rich without any spiritual help. All we are left with is positive thinking and a highly judgemental version of prosperity consciousness, where those who see that there is more to life than acquisitiveness are roundly vilified.

If you don't support the concept of hard work and wealth creation being the only virtue, you are seen as proposing a charter for the workshy welfare case. The idea that you might have found a way to bypass money on the way to fulfilment is inconceivable. It is also resented and resisted because it might undermine the threadbare belief system of the plutocracy.

As in so much of life at this turning point in our history, attitudes and beliefs have become polarised. You are either a rich stalwart of society or a poor excuse, a paragon of prosperity or a martyr to poverty. The subtle middle ground, where wealth is sometimes achieved as an incidental by-product of following your heart, is lost in the crossfire.

When we talk about 'acknowledging abundance' or 'manifestation', it seems it is very easy to be misunderstood. Even the concepts of 'positive thinking' and 'prosperity consciousness' have impeccable track-records, and are at the root of many of the most striking examples of 'right livelihood' today. The problem is that all these terms have been filched by people who are motivated by greed, insecurity, fear and the pomposity that comes from having deep-seated low self-esteem. Their façades are exquisitely constructed to give an appearance of self-assurance and solid integrity, but there is no heart there, no love and no feeling for abundance. If there were, why, then, would they need to accumulate money and things to prove they exist and have value?

No amount of money can create a feeling of abundance,

fulfilment or even wealth. Prosperity consciousness has nothing whatever to do with money or the accumulation of things. The confusion arises because those who open themselves to prosperity or abundance generally do have everything they need! This attracts those who see life and success in purely material terms. They latch on to the acquisition system without adopting the underlying philosophy, so terms that were once respectable become tawdry. 'Prosperity consciousness' is a case in point. As the term tends to be used now it has come to be synonymous with materialism. Those who use it have by and large lost their way. Will they ever realise that riches do not produce fulfilment, fun, happiness or anything else that makes life worth living?

'Prosperity consciousness today' (PCT, for short) says you can have whatever you *want* (usually money, material things and status symbols of various kinds). The case of Abundance, on the other hand, is that your *needs* are always met, and if what you need is to be patient and allow your Ego to give way to a higher consciousness, that is the need that will be met . . . 'Thy will, not mine be done'.

'PCT' says all that stands in your way to financial success is poverty consciousness. Yet the block to experiencing abundance is actually resistance to being yourself, growing and learning, aligning yourself, facing your shadows and coming into the light.

'PCT' says you can attract things as an end in themselves. Abundance argues that when you do this, you create a new pattern of life from which you may learn. If you're even a little bit wise, you can recognise how the pattern does not serve you and let go of it without wasting time and energy on the attraction process.

Let's look at Thomas's story. Thomas has experienced one financial disaster already. He lost £130,000 on a very dubious enterprise. Now he has lighted on a very worthwhile manufacturing project, bed-rests for the chronically ill at half the price of anything currently available. But he keeps being sucked into his old thinking. It is not enough to allow the business to grow organically. He has to sell thousands of bed-rests every week. Make millions. Employ lots of people. Be a big success. 'I want a comfortable life, not to have to think twice about buying whatever I want or going to the Bahamas', he says, 'I'm fed up with being poor and in debt.'

My task is to remind him that when his last venture was successful, his staff ripped him off. They resented his wealth and saw it as an excuse for stealing from him. And he was bored by it. So it fell apart. 'Why,' I ask him, 'are you setting out to create the same miserable pattern again? Why are you not looking at what in you denies you the right to feel good about yourself? What do you need to learn from the last experience in order to come through this one successfully?'

He has a wonderful opportunity to learn and grow in self-esteem. I cannot do it for him, but I can point out where he is setting up a repeat of his previous self-sabotage, and support him in letting go of the past and moving on to a more self-empowering future. You don't have to be rich to be a wonderful human being. You just have to find the courage to be real.

RESISTING THE TAUNTS

Money is very useful. It pays the rent. And 'PCT' feeds on this, and on the all-too-prevalent fear of not being able to pay the rent. The underlying fear is 'Loss of face' which, like so many other dreaded events, would actually be a glorious triumph. Loss of face really means loss of façade, the first step to becoming authentic and valuing yourself. But 'PCT' goes in the opposite direction. It says, 'Money is useful, so the more of it you can hoard the better'. This places an inappropriate and exaggerated importance on money as the sole aim in life and the answer to all life's problems. And because our society is so obsessed with money, this argument is very plausible.

Who doesn't want a few bob more?! Who hasn't got a bill to pay or a present to buy that a £50 note would greatly facilitate? Who doesn't occasionally get fed up deciding whether to buy a new pair of shoes or to spend a night at the Festival Hall? Of course you would like more money. If someone says, 'So why not join my get-rich-quick, money-making scheme?' is it really mealy-mouthed and judgemental to say, 'Because your scheme comes from a place I wouldn't want to come from. Because if I come on board, I take a step away from valuing my self for myself. Because if I really need shoes and a concert ticket, they're on their way. Because your scheme demands a degree of compromise that is not good for my soul.'

But an answer like this is nothing to the judgement you're likely to receive from the followers of 'PCT'.

Not to adopt their creed and try to join the well-heeled professionals their schemes attract is presented back to you as 'poverty consciousness'. 'You don't have very much self-esteem', they say, as if they knew what the word meant. And this is a shame because what they're selling may often be quite valuable – a route to health, interesting books, environmentally-friendly or improving products. However, all this is secondary in the 'PCT' book to the accumulation of conspicuous wealth. The smell of greed and insincerity taints the scheme.

Can you remain true to your self while all around you people are being economical with the truth, pressurising, overstating their case and glossing over any objections? It is a severe test of one's ability to operate ethically and with integrity . . . a major challenge for the individual working with spirit. Maintaining an ethical stance amidst all this glitz is to be applauded. It is a hard road.

What the 'PCT' adherents fail to recognise is that money is only of value if you value nothing else and that the pursuit of money as a primary objective diminishes rather than enhances self-esteem. This was the tragedy of the 1980s.

GUIDELINES FOR ETHICAL LIVING

How can you avoid compromising your ethics and integrity in the pursuit of the money and the resources you need to maintain yourself?

Here are some basic guidelines.

1. Don't hard sell. Don't push so hard that people go on the defensive, or feel embarrassed or awkward about saying no.

2. Hear when people are saying no and respect that.

3. If you had all the money you could possibly use, would you still be selling the product or service you sell? If not, stop selling it.

4. Don't be economical with the truth.

5. Don't associate with people whose sole objective is the accumulation of money. Avoid sales opportunity presentations where the primary appeal is to people's greed. It might rub off on you.

6. If the manufacturer's price is inflated, sell it for less, or stop selling it.

7. Listen to your intuition, and distinguish it from your Ego.

8. Connect with your core being, the essence of love in you and follow its promptings. Ask always what would love do?

9. Check that you feel good about yourself as you do your work, but not just *because* of your work.

10. Let your work be a primary way of loving and taking care of yourself. Put your labour where your love is.

The path of detachment

The balance that is vital to achieve in this is the balance of focus and detachment – first committing absolutely to a course of action and then releasing all attachment to the result. Attachment means you are dependent on the *results* of your work to restore or maintain your self-esteem. Attachment is Ego contamination. Attachment means the old rules apply and you will only get your result, if at all, by struggling and pushing. Get Ego out of the way, and you can have whatever you need . . . if you still actually need it!

The various techniques and systems that encourage people to focus on the results they want do have a place in achieving abundance, just as Napoleon Hill has a place. They are the scaffolding for the building of abundance. It is a step-by-step process. For someone who has never managed to have any real clarity about where they want to take their life, how they want to react to circumstances, the idea of focusing on results is excellent.

The next step is to investigate *why* those results are important. This can be done before or after achieving the desired result. Ask yourself what does the result achieve for me? Wealth? Security? Enhanced self-esteem? Relationship? A better job? A further sequence of questions should then follow. What is the wealth *for*? To feel good? To buy things to express feeling for others? To feel safe? To help others? Then these are the real results sought, and most of them do not require wealth or even money.

Why *do* I feel insecure? Why is my self-esteem below par? What difference *will* a new relationship or job make, if I don't love myself without them? You only discover the real vision, rather than the Ego-driven ambition, when the answers to the question 'Why?' are clearly faced, when there is complete commitment without attachment. This tends to mean that unless the process and the result you seek is personal growth, any apparent progress is a mirage and there is only stagnation.

Struggle free or struggle-free?

Are you going to struggle to get free or is your life going to be struggle-free? The new way of working with money and resources is so different from the experience of those who work with outmoded attitudes to money. These outmoded ways constantly affirm lack and separation. There is never enough to go round and money is hard to come by. Whereas *we* now know that what makes it hard is resistance and negative belief. The old attitude to money states that needs can only be met by hard work and struggle, and if needs are not being met, then the answer must be to work harder and struggle harder. The idea that enjoying yourself might be a better route to having your needs met is unthinkable in the old paradigm, and yet it is the truth of the new.

Fear, anxiety, tension, worry – all run rampant in the language of industry and commerce. Money becomes the repository for all the bad feelings we have about ourselves. It is where all our negative attitudes to self, work, success, plans and life in general surface. We can either keep feeding this negativity and repressing it as Napoleon Hill and his descendants propose, or we can be truly courageous, face it and start living.

Potential energy

The tragedy is that the new principles of money are so much easier and more effective than the old and probably a large part of the reason why they work so well is because the result no longer matters so much. The new principles of money start working for you the moment you let go all your attachment to anything outside yourself to validate you. Money, the things it buys and all other resources are no longer seen as external, something to be attracted to you, something you need be open to receive. With the new principles of abundance we are working on a much bigger canvas, creating a whole new consciousness, where there is no separation between me and other, me and it, me and money. Money and the other resources we need to support ourselves are more like potential energy, stored within us; all we have to do is find ways to release them and allow them to surface.

This requires a total change in attitude to life, where life happens *for* me, not *to* me. There is nothing 'out there' that I have to fight for or with. There is nothing I have to play 'pretty please' with. I am not in competition to get a bigger piece of the pie, rather there is no distinction between me and the pie. It is all there already – all I have to do is recognise it and manifest what already exists, like heat, lying as potential, waiting to be discovered within coal.

In exactly the same way that we all have the potential for

unconditional love, if we dig deep enough under all the layers of superficiality and self-vilification, so money and everything else is also waiting there as potential energy, lurking beneath all the feelings of lack and separation. If I look for love *or* money outside myself, and even if I think I have found it, I still have all those layers of low self-esteem and feelings of inadequacy to look at, then resolve and release. This is why relationships go wrong when we see the attraction of someone else's love as a way of avoiding work on our own personal growth, and in exactly the same way this is why accumulating piles of money without ever dealing with the feelings of low self-esteem is desperately unsatisfying, a huge anticlimax.

Get it right on the inner

As long as we go on looking to external sources of money as the solution to all our problems, it – money – will continue to be there as an unending and hilarious series of lessons, though *we* may not see the funny side. And most of us have to go through the painful process of trying to accumulate money from 'out there' and love from 'out there' before we can learn that we were looking in the wrong place. When you are in a good connection with yourself, when you are in the right place, doing the right thing, being the right way, when everything is right on the spiritual level, then everything comes right on the financial level, the physical level. Getting everything right on the purely physical, financial level, however, does absolutely nothing for you at the spiritual level. Most of us just have to experience that in order to find the truth in it. Many, sadly, never even get to the point of accumulating enough to know that there is never enough to resolve things that way. When things are not working out on the physical, financial level, this is merely an indication that there is work to be done at some other level and this work, without exception, will start by checking how things stand at the spiritual level.

People often come to The Breakthrough Centre with money worries. Dorothy, for instance, makes beautiful quilts. Things were just not adding up financially and she could see no way out as the debt accumulated. So we talked and gradually over two or three months she rediscovered her enthusiasm for what she was doing. She also faced up to what it would mean to let it all go, and having considered the prospect found that she could value herself and her work so highly that it could obviously be a crime to give it up. So she put all her energy into it and was open to whatever needed to happen. Orders started to flow again. Shops made contact and even paid up. As things improved, her self-image also improved and her new inner attitude affected her outer reality.

Donald's business had run into serious trouble. In the end the only way out was to come to an agreement with his creditors. The sense of relief was immense. He had expected to feel devastated by the admission of failure. Instead, he found a new sense of self within and was able to come closer to who he really was and what would reflect his real self most satisfactorily in the outer world. Relations started to help and he set up a new business network that enabled others to invest in him. Even now there are problems, always created by allowing the outer realities to suppress the inner truths. When he remembers and realises this, the inner resolution works through to the outer.

Patrick lost his job and was for a time very confused and hurt. But he had always put his Inner Self first and over the years, this trust in something beyond understanding inspired him through thick and thin to build a centre that attracts large numbers of people every year. Whatever it needs is attuned to on the inner and released to come in the form it needs to come at the right time.

The real test for all of them is how they react when things *don't* work out. Do they agonise about the outer, or hold on to the strength that comes from inner trust? There are more lessons when things don't work out than when they do. Listening to the feedback is a primary lesson.

Hearing the feedback

Perhaps your vision is out of alignment. Perhaps there are others you need to involve, without whom the vision cannot be realised. Perhaps the form you are working with is inappropriate. And perhaps you have now finished with this particular stage and it is time to move on. Or perhaps it is a test of your commitment, or a way for the Universe to give you feedback on your (lack of) commitment level.

Let's look at another couple of stories. Neville was having difficulties in his relationship at home. His wife Shona was impossible to please, disgruntled, and turned down every suggestion Neville made. He was trying to resolve this with presents, nights out, and logical responses to her outbursts. But he wasn't really hearing what was being said, and he was stubbornly refusing to allow his emotions and his own feelings for himself to be engaged. The realisation that what he had to do was look at what *in him* interlocked with Shona's unhappiness came as a shock. He started slowly to admit to feeling sad, neglected and unchallenged. 'So who is best placed to acknowledge, care for and assure you?' we asked. It took several sessions and groups, but in the end we got the right answer, 'Me . . . I suppose'. We have yet to see how things will proceed with Shona, but Neville is allowing more of his playful, loving, amusing child to come out, and I have no doubt this is the only route that has any mileage. Whether they stay together or not Neville will emerge as Neville.

Loren has been trying to work up enthusiasm for his work and indeed for his life for months. Just the other day he announced 'I'm not going to struggle any more.' He had learnt the lesson from his struggle to get his life together – struggling doesn't work. Now the way is open to try a different tack. There are many possibilities. There may be many things to let go. He may need to give more time and attention to inner worth. And he may even be called on to put a lot of effort into activity. But not struggle. What enters his life instead is beauty and joy.

These are very personal stories. Your own story will be different. Are you clear what the feedback is on your life? Are you hearing it? Are you reacting to it and embracing the next step forward? Or are you resisting it and creating an even bigger, louder blast of feedback to present itself? Be still and listen. Your inner voice will help you get where you need to be.

A marker not a measure

Like everything else in your life, money and the way it works for you and you work with it, is there as a lesson. That's all it's for, it doesn't prove anything, it doesn't validate anything, it doesn't have any meaning or value in itself. It is just a marker, and you ignore it at your peril. When money flows freely through your life, or your business, it is a clear sign that you have been willing to release and realise your potential to enter into a co-creative partnership with the Divine Essence. It is not the only sign of this; indeed it is probably the least significant sign of this, but if it is not actively present in your life, it is worth checking very carefully before assuming that you may act with disdainful superiority towards it.

If money really is unimportant to you, well done! If this is the case all your needs are met on a daily basis and you will view with love, care and sympathy those who are still working with it. But if you claim that money is unimportant to you and then get angry with those who suggest that this is just a cop out because you can't make any, or the outward and visible sign of your poverty consciousness and low self-esteem, then you are not complete with money. Those who are complete with it recognise and value those who are not yet complete and see that they too are on the path to enlightenment. Furthermore, if you are complete with money and have cracked this particular lesson, you will be happy to drop a few hints about the easier principles you have discovered for those who are still struggling with the old laws. You may be sure they are only working with them because it hasn't occurred to them that there might be another way.

Working with trust and self-esteem

Using money as just a measure of wealth, let alone of abundance, is like using an expensive computer as a doorstop. It does the job very effectively and with a certain style, but it is wholly under-potentialised. So it is with money. It is very much more useful and valuable than its simple face value. Money is an extremely sophisticated tool for working with trust and self-esteem.

When you have it:

- Can you continue to trust that it will not desert you?
- Can you remain open to returning to a life without it?
- Can you settle for what you have, and not keep looking for even more?
- Can you freely share it unconditionally with others? How much? Ten, twenty, fifty, ninety per cent?
- Can you still maintain a simple, inconspicuous lifestyle?
- Can you still value yourself for who you are rather than what you've got?
- Can you value *others* for themselves and not for what they have and haven't got?
- Can you avoid invidious comparisons?
- Can you still take risks?
- Can you be a good custodian?
- Can you feel abundant?

When you don't have it:

- Can you trust that all your needs will be met?
- Can you love and value yourself unconditionally?
- Can you be happy and content, living like a lord on very little?
- Can you still be a go-giver?
- Can you stick to your principles?
- Can you invest in yourself and your growth?
- Can you feel good in rich, expensive company?
- Can you receive gifts and charity without humiliation, pride or resentment?
- Can you give your time, money and energy to others unstintingly?
- Can you allow money to flow through you?
- Are you a good custodian of the little you do have?
- Can you still recognise the boundless abundance around and inside you?

Entering abundance

There are lessons to learn whether you have money or not. It hardly matters. The lessons are different, that's all. If you don't learn them one way, you'll probably get to learn them another way. What those lessons are, how you might react to them, what changes you can make and what action you can take to enter abundance is the subject matter for the rest of this book.

You can have no money and feel abundant. You can have loads of money and not feel abundant. And of course you *can* be rich and feel abundant all at the same time. Or you can feel poor and unabundant too: in that case you tend to stay that way. Money and abundance are on two completely separate scales.

In the graph on page 84, Point A represents someone who has piles of money and has still not learnt to trust in the abundance of the universe. He or she will keep seeking to accumulate more and more in a desperate effort to feel safe. This is the tragedy of so many C2 voters, for example, who use money as the sole measure of self-value, and set themselves on a treadmill which never gives them their own power. The greatest Point A 'success story' of recent times was Robert Maxwell. Had he lived he would have come to experience Point B.

Point B represents the people who have no resources and believe the Universe is against them. Their belief systems keep them poor, and there is nothing one can do for them, until they begin to acknowledge, then value and then love themselves for who they are. Point A people make heavy judgements of Point B people, but Point B is just a place to be and learn about abundance, just as much as any other point on the chart. In some ways it is easier to discover abundance at Point B than anywhere else because you cannot use money to confuse the issue. There isn't any. So your way is clear to value yourself, unhampered by the distractions of money, and move to Point C.

At Point C, you still have no money, but feel wealthy because you love yourself unconditionally and appreciate the little you have even more than Point A person appreciate the pile that they have. Your needs are few and tend to be met, because you trust. And the chances are that if you need more resources to support your vision, you will move towards Point D and find that you are showered with abundance.

Point D is not the perfect place. To experience abundance at its ultimate does not require great wealth. Anywhere between C and D is fine, and wherever you are between those two points you will be growing and learning about abundance. Prosperity consciousness is only concerned with arriving between A and D. Abundance is blissfully happy and fulfilled anywhere between C and D.

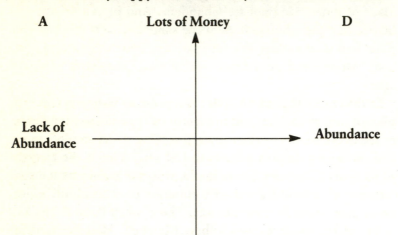

If you do not trust and believe in your own innate worth, it won't matter how far you climb up the money axis. You still won't acknowledge your abundance. But if you pursue the path of self-awareness and discovery, you will start shifting into abundance. This inevitably opens you up to being showered with pennies from heaven, not to mention love, appreciation and gifts.

The old laws affirm lack and separation: they have you always looking outside to get what you want to feed your needy Ego. The new laws affirm connection with abundance: they have you looking *inside* to acknowledge all you need is there waiting for you. The door is open. Come on in.

Money is only of value if you value nothing else.

5

—•—

The Only Problem is Interference

ABUNDANCE is about your reaction to what life gives you, whether you believe it is out to get you or is on your side. Where do these different attitudes come from?

What interferes with the creation of abundance? What stops you along the path from vision to action? What are the blocks that get in the way? What is it we need to change and move through in order to enter abundance?

The main obstacles in work, business or any aspect of life are essentially personal, individual and psychological. There are no obstacles 'out there', only resistances in each of us to overcoming or coping with them. Rather than bemoaning the lack of imagination or entrepreneurship in banks and the bureaucracy, it is more productive to take responsibility for the situation. It's easy to create a problem with the bank or the revenue, or an employer, but why do that? Why not adopt a stance that is both positive and realistic, and recognise that resistance from any quarter is a sign that you may not yet have it right? Everything that happens happens for a reason; there are lessons to be learned. Resistance, wherever it comes from, can simply indicate there is something you need to look at. It may be a sort of test that you create because you are anxious about moving forward. It can be a temporary check that you are really serious, and a test of your resolve and intention.

It is worth recognising when you are resisting and studying

the reasons why. We each have our own ways and reasons to fail or block success. This happens at the corporate level as well as at the individual level. Corporations and groups are made up of individuals. If the individuals are resisting progress and change, this is reflected in the way the group works. Your responsibility is not to be part of that blocking process, but to be on the side of the angels. The only thing that stands between you and abundance is *you*. And the best way to connect with you is to be still and listen.

GETTING IT WRONG

Moving from the known to the unknown, from the tried and tested to the strange and new is something we are quite naturally reluctant to do, and yet unless we do it this reluctance becomes a major barrier to growth and perhaps even survival. It has never been more important for us to understand why we resist change and how we can come to terms with it. It involves stepping out of the comfortable world of 'We've always done it that way' into the less comfortable world where 'I might get this wrong'.

At the root of most resistance to change is the reluctance to make mistakes, and yet we need to recognise that the person who never made a mistake probably never made anything.

You will have experienced your own resistance when reading this and other such books. At some point I can almost guarantee you hear a voice from somewhere saying, 'Who do you think you are?' and at times I can be almost as certain there is a voice saying, 'And who does he think he is?' Other voices will have said, 'I can't do anything about it. I can't make a difference. I don't matter. It's somebody else's problem.' That kind of thinking got us into the mess we are in and it's going to take every single one of us to get out of it. If you're not putting in your two penn'orth you're part of the problem.

A LONG HISTORY OF RESISTANCE

So, let's take a look at what is involved in overcoming resistance and managing change so we can grow into abundance. We will review our approaches to change and acknowledge how we have successfully negotiated change in the past and use this to understand both what gets in the way and how to accelerate progress. Your worst fears about this are almost certainly unfounded. In a few minutes you will have the reassurance that it is safe to be you, safe to take a stand, safe to enter abundance.

A shift in energy levels has to take place. We have the possibility and the responsibility to stop undermining ourselves and instead to allow abundance. It is time to ease ourselves out of blocked energy and into a relationship with ourselves, which we can carry into the work we do and the organisations where we do it.

For example, Laura was absolutely exhausted by the situation at work when I met her. She had tried to be nice and helpful and amenable to clients who were raising objections to paying for services received. She suppressed her own needs and wants, and allowed herself to be distracted from the main aim of the operation. She managed, and gave most of her time to responding to her debtors' demands. They resisted valuing her service, and she responded by confirming their evaluation and trying to make it right for them. But this went on for two years. Each time she put something right, the clients dreamt up new complaints. Clearly their game was not to get it right, but to avoid payment. Equally clearly, as long as Laura didn't value her service and herself, neither would they.

Her fear was that if she insisted on her needs being met, the way the clients insisted on their needs being met, they would become hostile and she would no longer be seen as nice and amenable. Her task was to realise that there is a difference between being amenable and being a doormat. The whole situation was set up as a test. Would she put her foot down and risk their hostility? Or would she continue to believe that she was only loved and lovable if she was nice and amenable? Would she have the courage to express her anger and resentment, or would she suppress them and take refuge in hopelessness?

Over a six-month period, she made the shift. She decided with the rest of her team what was and was not reasonable. She made clear what she was going to do to keep her side of the bargain, and took professional advice on how to ensure the other parties kept their side of the bargain. Having completed what all agreed was sufficient, and found the clients still refusing to pay, she started legal proceedings, content that if all else failed, the clients would still be sacked.

This was the outer action, and the result hardly mattered. It is in progress so we will have to wait and see. What does matter is the inner shift. Although the whole situation is much more tense and threatening, Laura is relaxed, glowing, and her own person. She has stopped being stopped by people who feel they have a hold over her. Instead she is standing her own ground, still as nice as ever, but no longer prepared to have her helpfulness abused. Hope has replaced hopelessness, and she is actively pursuing the real vision of her operation. I was reminded at this point in the saga that Laura is 29 – the classic age to make a break from received philosophies and become oneself. She's doing fine!

So what is it that gets in the way? Why do we sometimes act or react in a way that is unproductive? We have already looked at some of the old patterns we have been acting out and this is one place to look for answers. They result in our feeling unworthy or not good enough. They leave us with a church mouse mentality or poverty consciousness and the unshakeable belief that money and resources are always in short supply. They make us defensive, waiting for things to go wrong, so that they always do. This is what runs our lives and lays down the rules by which organisations are run. This is why it is almost dangerous to question assumptions about growth and the accumulation of profits. Such questions undermine the basic belief systems by which people live their lives. Without them they fear life will end, whereas in fact the opposite is true. Life will end *unless* we let go of them. The world of work is not just a place to get the money to live on, it is also the place where the future of the planet is being decided. The work you do and the way you do it either contribute to destruction or salvation.

There isn't really a choice, is there? And yet there is still resistance and defensiveness.

Intimate confessions

To let go of the assumptions we make about abundance and prosperity seems to imply self-condemnation. This is strange when all it is is the process of education, of learning better ways to do things. There is nothing to hide, nothing to be ashamed of. If we all confessed our faults, crimes and shortcomings, the most we could be accused of is a lack of originality. At the bottom line we are all the same. We all have the same negative core belief chipping away.

Releasing these negative core beliefs is a five-stage process. Suppose the bottom line for you is 'I'm no good'. You will not, incidentally, be alone in this. Somewhere deep down just about everyone has this belief. The effect it has on them, whether it destroys them or not, depends on what they do with it. To avoid self-destruction, this is what you do.

1. Allow the feeling to be there. Don't fight it or resist it. It is part of you, not all of you, so it's safe to allow that part to be there. If you disallow it, it will find ways to get back at you, to prove it's true. It will keep creating situations where you can foul up, be rejected and wallow in self-pity.

2. Listen to the feeling. Hear it saying 'You're no good'. Encourage it to expand on its theme, giving you chapter and verse, the reasons why it feels this and where those feelings come from.

3. Acknowledge the feeling. Reassure that part of yourself that you know it's there and that it has a right to be there. The formula to use is simple. 'It's OK that I'm no good.' You connect with it when you do this and it becomes less anxious to express itself. As with any objection, only $\frac{1}{10}$ is real objection; the other $\frac{9}{10}$ is the result of not having been consulted.

4. Raise the feeling to a higher level. Having acknowledged the feeling, it can become less demoralised and demoralising. 'I'm no good and that's OK' becomes 'I could be better, and that's OK.' This in turn becomes 'Sometimes I am better, and that's OK', and then 'I'm good in parts' and 'part of me is good'. At this point 'I am a good person' is as true as 'I'm no good'. And then if that is true, it is also true that I am great, wonderful, inspiring and a being filled with divine energy . . . and that's OK!

5. As you raise the level, resistance can rear its head again! 'Wonderful? Me?' Yes, this also is your truth, and it is important to allow, hear and acknowledge any resistance to this. The fifth step is to persist through the resistance, without suppressing the resistance.

This five-step process draws on Harley Miller's Quality Cards which provide practical examples of a number of negative core beliefs you can raise to a higher level.

Those most intimate and personal feelings that you have about yourself, that you scarcely dare to admit even to yourself, are the feelings that we all have. Carl Rogers put it very neatly when he said, 'The more intimate or personal a feeling is that you have about yourself, the more universal it is'. All the blocks we have to change flow from these primeval musts and shoulds. The very language we use is littered with subtle negatives. Words are often in disguise and there is actually a different music playing in the background. What for instance is a 'serious relationship'? Serious, heavy, ponderous, joyless? So any relationship I am in that gets 'serious' loses all the fun and joy. Many words and ideas imply failure and block success; they need converting to more positive expressions. You will be familiar with most or all of them. By calling something a problem we make it a problem, instead of a challenge or an opportunity, bearing a gift of knowledge and wisdom. Look at how reluctant we are to stop using the word 'but' and replace it with 'and'. When we 'try' to do something 'hopefully' we are actually saying we will try and we will fail, that we hope it will happen, but we actually believe it won't. And we are actually setting up for it to be OK for it not to work. Using the word 'intend' instead of 'try' or 'hope' changes all that. When you say 'if only' you reinforce the fact that it is not. Try saying 'let's pretend' or 'suppose' – that's a little better. In the end, just be clear that you intend what you suppose.

Don't say you're working 'hard'. Work 'well' instead. Nothing is difficult, which does not mean that everything is easy. It may take a little time, and that is all. Even the word 'no' needs to be translated. In Hindi there is no word for 'no'; they say, 'Not yet'. In other words 'Yes, soon'.

'I can't do it' means the same as 'I won't do it' – and both mean, 'I have chosen positively not to do it'. Probably the commonest excuse is 'I didn't have time'. Nonsense! You had all the time in the world, you just chose not to do it because it was not a priority for you.

Let's start being honest with ourselves and with each other. The social niceties have no place here. People are not 'unlucky', they choose not to receive, and they have no excuse for saying they don't know something when the truth is that they chose to ignore it.

Many people will already be familiar with these ideas. Putting them into practice in the working environment is a bit more of a challenge. Knowing the rules does not make you immune to them. And as they say in North Dublin 'Denial is not a river in Egypt!'

What you have to do is use language consciously. Avoid negative expressions that disempower you. Stop stopping yourself with words, and remove 'but', 'try', 'can't' 'hard', 'hope' and so on from your vocabulary.

AFFIRMING THE POSITIVE

So what else will help you get out of your own way? A good next step is to recognise that life works extremely well when you do get out of your own way. The successes you have already achieved in your life and your work happened because your positive side was not being undermined by the negative core beliefs you carry around with you. So keep affirming the positive and asserting yourself. Remind yourself constantly that the Universe is a safe and friendly place. It is not out to get you. This process of affirmation really can reprogramme your subconscious so that you no longer suffer a lack of self-esteem, which makes you a loser. Let life happen *for* you, not *to* you.

Saying 'Yes!' to life, 'Yes, I love myself!' and in George Trevelyan's phrase, 'I am a droplet of Divinity', and 'No, I am not prepared to accept the negative or the pressures I have put myself under', all help to affirm the positive side of you instead of reinforcing and feeding negativity.

It is important to do something about doing something. The only wrong decision is no decision. You may waste a little time, but you are more likely to learn something. As long as you did something you did not decide wrongly. Having faith that something will happen is not the same as sitting back in a warm bath of complacency and lazily assuming it will. And having patience is not the same thing as being passive.

Later in the book, in Chapter 9, we look at the action required to shift your belief systems. Meanwhile we focus on what might be going on and how it might be different. If you are itching to get into action, there is no harm in taking a peek at Chapter 9 now and beginning to work on the first action points suggested there.

Fear and excitement are almost the same thing. Fear is leaning away from life, away from choice. Excitement is leaning towards life, towards choice. Fear is frozen excitement. When you stop being excited about something there is no need to be fearful, it just means it is time to move on. So allow time and space in your life to allow new things to come in. Don't be so busy that good things can't find their way in. Don't keep your pot so full of fear that no new energy can get into it. If you have a pot of love and keep sharing it, it will keep getting filled up. If you fill it with fear, defensiveness and competitiveness, nothing can get in, and that's how you get stuck. Even simple things like having a clear out – getting rid of old clothes, tapes, possessions, grudges – makes space for new energy and new things to come in. If I may be forgiven for getting biblical for a moment, 'To him that hath [love, energy flowing in abundance] shall be given [love, energy]. From him that hath not [love] shall be taken even that which he hath. [The energy stored up in possessions.]'

Willingness to receive

We receive constant feedback on what we are doing, if only we can hear it. It's like driving a car. Ninety per cent of the time you are off course, so you keep adjusting the steering. If you don't take note of your own feedback you will run into a tree – and that's real feedback! We are not very good at it. Think of the engine and systems of an aeroplane on auto-pilot. The auto-pilot is constantly telling you you are off course and the aeroplane's systems respond without demur, but human beings start to get cross after just a couple of pieces of feedback. Every time you miss the feedback it gets louder. The technical terminology for this is 'sledgehammer guidance'.

Let's take a look at Ian, who prided himself on working a 75-hour week to provide a comfortable lifestyle for his family. He was becoming increasingly dependent on alcohol to handle the shift from work to home, and never realised that his dependency indicated something was wrong. What he really wanted was to go back into full-time education, but he never discussed this with his family because he assumed they wanted the comfortable life. A short affair failed to get through to him that his lifestyle was false and shallow. Still he kept his wishes to himself. Then his daughter contracted meningitis, and at last his priorities changed, and he and his wife started to communicate. He was amazed to find she supported his long-suppressed desire.

Then there was Zoe who lived on her nerves, obsessed with growing a business and turning over a million. Those who worked for her were terrified of her, and there was nobody in her life. So she had to take all the decisions and could rely on no one. Her nerves were raw. But she was too obsessed with growth to hear the feedback and read the symptoms. Now she has M.E., and there has been no one to continue the business. At last she has slowed down.

Both of the above are cases of sledgehammer guidance finally making itself heard after subtle symptoms were ignored. Neither would have dreamed of seeking advice.

A large part of getting out of your own way is not just about giving and doing, it's about being willing to receive – not just what you ask for because you always get what you need, and there is always a lesson about what you asked for. What you get may well not be what you asked for because you didn't really need it – money, a new sweater, an easy success – or it may not yet be time. Have robust expectancy but no expectations. Expectations are blinkers – they stop you seeing the possibilities that were beyond your comprehension.

The degree to which you are interested in other people is a good indicator of your own opinion of yourself and how that may get in your way.

Quiz
Score yourself from 0–10 on each of these questions. 0 means Strongly No and 10 means Strongly Yes.

	0	1	2	3	4	5	6	7	8	9	10
Do you see the best in others?											
Do you love and care for them?											
Do you give gracefully to them?											
Do you share your judgements of others with them?											
Do you find others inspiring, amusing, thrilling?											
Do you like being with people?											

Low scores obviously indicate a shy, defensive, over self-conscious attitude which is the stuff of low personal self-esteem. Inability to love and give to others or be excited by them goes hand in hand with reluctance to love yourself.

High scores can indicate that you use other people to avoid being self-reliant, and they too suggest you may have difficulty valuing yourself. Seeing the best in others is fine, as long as you see the best in yourself too. Loving, giving to others and being excited by them in strong measure can be a way of dumping yourself on others and not valuing yourself. As for judgement, the only person you ever judge is yourself! A score somewhere between 4 and 6 is probably about right.

MAKING CHANGES

Let's pause for a moment and look at what the changes are that you want to make in your life. The current stone in your shoe, a major shift in emphasis, whatever will allow abundance to flow. If you can share this with someone you trust, so much the better. Get them to keep asking you, 'What do you *really* want to change, and why?' and ask them to write down what is coming up. So often we get into dealing with the superficialities, the presenting problem, instead of getting at the cause, the real issue that needs to be addressed.

Here are some more questions:

- What seems to be the problem? What's the block?
- What's stopping you?
- How do you resist change?
- What do you need to do to get change to happen for you?
- How will that change increase your abundance?
- Is it really the major change?

An important step in the abundance process is seeing what will make a real difference, what form the interference takes. When you start to look at this a critical path for change will often emerge, with a chain of issues that are all inter-connected.

Simply wrestling with the presenting problem will get you nowhere because the difficulty has its roots elsewhere. Some of the people close to you may not be helping and everything in the end can be traced back to a block in yourself. This is what you really need to look at – not the superficial circumstances, but YOU.

Through the comfort zone

When you accept this and start to work with it, the resistance other people have stops interlocking with your own resistance. It's uncomfortable – it involves moving out of what is comfortable for you, what is familiar, your comfort zone – so of course there's resistance. Change is growth, is change. It is how we face our dragons and grow. It is how we move from the known to the unknown. Clear aims are crucial because growth without aims will probably lead to an even bigger mess, and growth that doesn't integrate you at the deepest level makes you less of yourself, whereas work is meant to be a place to grow, not to wither.

All it takes is your resolution to face the challenges and act on the blocks, otherwise frustration and distress is all there is. The blocks to change are always in us, they are never anywhere else. Once we know and understand why we resist change we can change that too. In any situation there will be a part of us that wants – for instance to move forward, to let go – and part of us that resists. So there is a conflict and this can be going on deep in the subconscious. We have already looked at some of the failure scripts that stop people stepping into their potential: the belief, for instance, that successful people aren't quite nice; that if I am successful other people will resent it; that accepting compliments or laying claim to success (without of course rubbing other people's noses in it) are arrogance by any other name. People believe they simply can't hack it, they always come second. They buy into the idea that the higher you go, the harder you fall, so you'd better not go too high. They accept too readily the drip-feed of negative suggestions and school reports and end up believing that because everybody always said I'd never make it, I probably won't. Or they fight against this in a distorted way – 'I'll show them!' – and of course all they show is that those people were right.

How can you face a blocking belief system like this and let go of it? Here is another approach. Have pen and paper beside you and take yourself off to a quiet, relaxed space. Connect with the voice inside you that always says 'I can't . . .'. Listen to how it sabotages you and write down the self-defeating messages that come from this part of you.

Return to quietness and contact the voice inside that supports you and says 'I can ...'. Listen to what this part of you says and write it down.

Take another few moments of quiet to let the supportive 'I can ...' voice speak to the sabotaging 'I can't ...'. Then take each of your 'I can't ... statements in turn and write down the most positive 'I can ...' replies to them.

Select from all these statements the 'Greatest Lie,' the positive statement you have the greatest difficulty accepting, and resolve to work with it. You will probably feel stronger already, and will have moved at least some distance into 'I can ...'. Don't make the mistake of feeling that you are shouting down your sabotaging self. You are simply balancing things up. If you *suppress* the negative, it returns to haunt you. If you engage in a balanced dialogue it can be won over and 'I can ...' becomes a more prevailing reality than 'I can't ...'.

Be prepared for feedback, resistance and events that undermine your positivity, and return to this exercise each time it happens. It's taken you 30 or 40 years to create your current state of mind. Changing it may take more than 30 or 40 minutes!

SELF-SABOTAGE

I have watched people dismantle an inevitable success systematically. They put tremendous energy into building up a business, setting everything up with remarkable tenacity and determination, and then just at the point that it is about to be successful, they start taking it to pieces, dismantling it, destroying it. I have been with salesmen in the field who have done a copybook job on getting a really substantial order, only to sabotage themselves as they are leaving by putting doubts into the customer's mind about whether the order will actually be delivered or whether it will be exactly what they thought, just in case something goes wrong. They have a belief system that nothing ever works for them − so when something does they have to destroy it otherwise the belief system which rules their life would fall away and their life would suddenly have no structure, no security. It is not that uncommon − it may well be a familiar scenario to you.

Each of us has a unique and very personal viewpoint, a way of perceiving reality. We see the world through rose-coloured, grey or almost completely black spectacles. This viewpoint is determined by conclusions we have reached and beliefs now stored in our subconscious. This is the way it is. And from that point on we attract situations that confirm this, because anything else means going back to square one and starting again, and there is no guarantee that square one will still be there or that we can ever find square two again.

Not everybody suffers from slow payment and bad debts. In my experience only about 10 per cent of businesses have a real problem with bad debts. I had a short string of bad debts myself about six years ago, and when I looked at it and wondered why it was happening I realised that I saw every one of them coming. I knew in advance who would and would not pay on time or at all, and yet I accepted the work and did my best with it. So six years ago I decided I didn't need bad debts any more. I didn't need to prove that people can't be trusted, or that my work did not have value. If I had any doubt about a new client, I politely but firmly asked for payment in two or three instalments, one payment to be made before work began. Most people paid without demur. A very few raised noisy objections. I didn't work with them, because their objections confirmed my suspicions. They weren't intending to pay. In practice I didn't press those who passed the test for early payment. I conceded to payment on or shortly after delivery. Since then I have not had a single bad debt and few people have taken more than 30 days to pay me.

At the time of writing, the percentage of people suffering seriously from bad debts may have doubled. Many have become desperate and, in order to win any business, allow fear to rule, instead of trusting intuition and common sense, even taking on business that is not worth having, thus aggravating this situation.

Bad debts and where it often leads, bankruptcy, are good places to learn lessons about self, self-esteem and what attachments undermine you. Will you value yourself so little that you work for no reward? It would be better to make a gift of the work in the first place, since the purchaser is clearly blocking his ability to receive and therefore give payment himself. If your soul needs you to experience bankruptcy in order to learn that a change of direction is needed, or that you have become complacent, or that you need to value yourself freed from the distraction of possessions which possess you ... you'll experience it.

Bad debt and bankruptcy is more widespread because our society has failed to learn abundance and is blind to the destruction and human misery its drive for mere prosperity creates around the world. As a society we have not paid a fair price for what we have taken from others. Indeed, we charge usurious amounts of interest on the money the Third World has borrowed, because we didn't pay them. We have left a trail of bankrupt people in our wake. Now we get to experience it ourselves. If we care for our *own* bankrupts, we may be allowed to step back from the brink. Meanwhile, a growing percentage of us have to experience it. In anticipation, it looks like the end of the world. In retrospect it can be releasing and re-empowering.

It's the same with unreliable suppliers, fickle lovers – whatever each of us feels we need to keep creating in order to confirm the rules we established for ourselves in our first three to seven years of life.

THE OVERPOPULATED VILLAGE

Inside each of us is a whole village of personalities – Mum, Dad, the reactions you had to them, the little boy, the clever little professor, the victim, the rebel, Jack the Lad, and some even older scripts, beliefs and romantic ideals such as the prince, princess, Santa Claus, the ogre.

One of the most difficult questions for me to answer is, 'How are you today?' I can give a quick, socially acceptable, unconsidered reply, 'I'm fine – how are you?' but if I really answer the question properly I need to check in with my village of personalities; I need to hold a council meeting. How are we all? How are you? How's the 'little professor' today? How's 'Jack the Lad'? How's the 'droplet of Divinity'? And once I have answers from all of them I can report back, '25 per cent of us feel a bit under the weather, and 75 per cent of us feel absolutely wonderful, so we're about 25/75 today, thanks very much.' Funnily enough I actually find people are far more satisfied with this answer than the superficial social answer.

It's only part of us that resists, and it's like a golden ball we drag around at the end of a golden chain. It has been well polished over the years, it's a beautiful thing, and it's hardly surprising there is reluctance to let it go. And let it go we must as we choose to exhibit other parts of ourselves more often. Once we recognise it and decide not to be stopped by it any more – without of course ignoring it and listening to the lessons and feedback it has to give us – we can move forwards. We can make the changes that enable us to grow; we can remove the blocks that stunt our growth.

CHOOSING ABUNDANCE

Take a few moments to jot down (1) the change you want to make – for instance, I want to be abundant; (2) the block to that change – for instance, the belief that I don't deserve it; and (3) the belief system that creates the block – fundamentally, when I get down to it I'm not good enough. That's the real block, that's what really gets in the way, and no amount of clever footwork, brilliant CVs and hard work will get me what I seek unless I look at the fundamental belief system I am working with. Guess at what the block might be if it's not obvious, and look at when, where and how it may have started. Ask yourself what seems to get in the way, what happens when you set out to be positive or make a change, what sabotages you, what exactly the 'I can't . . .' voice inside is saying. And think back to when it was first the truth for you. Recognise that it probably wasn't the truth then and it absolutely certainly isn't the truth now — so it's time to let go of it.

Your reaction to this suggestion may be to be nonplussed by it. It really does help to start telling somebody else. Your own head may stop you getting anywhere. So share what you've written with someone you trust. (Now why wouldn't you trust? What's the resistance to trust?) This time ask them to listen as you tell them what you've written, and listen in total silence, without any facial expression, without nodding, moving, encouraging, reaching out to touch you. Just ask them to feel love for you, to feel unconditional love for you, no matter what you say. Give yourself 10 minutes to do this. Once you have moved on from the change you want to make, to the block to that change, don't go back to talking about the change you want to make. Keep moving forward. By the same token, when you get to the belief system that creates the block, don't move back to talking about the block, keep moving forward. If that means you have to sit in silence for nine minutes, so be it. It may be the most powerful nine minutes of your life. Enjoy it!

Once you have completed your task — good! Now we can begin to disempower all that nonsense and empower you. Once you take responsibility not only can you choose to change, you have chosen. As long as you externalise, look for excuses outside yourself and gripe and moan, there is no hope for you, you have chosen to stay miserable, unemployed, whatever. It is your choice whether you empower yourself and grow, or disempower yourself and stagnate. The discomfort of undergoing change is nothing compared to the pain of resisting it.

A major part of achieving change is also about not resisting, allowing your conscious mind to acknowledge the subconscious script, 'Yes, I hear you, and I have decided that is no longer the truth. The content was unpleasant, it hurt, but the context has changed; I am no longer a sad little girl, or a carbon copy of my alcoholic father. It doesn't have to be that way any more.' The subconscious may still fight back, but just keep listening, acknowledging and choosing to change. You're in charge. No one else is doing it to you. It's your decision and your choice. Take 10 minutes every day to listen to the old belief and balance it with an empowering new belief.

Success comes in cans

There are no 'can'ts' remember. You may *choose* not to, but 'can't' is meaningless. As the saying goes, 'Success comes in cans not can'ts!' and if you want to change the world first change yourself, and if you don't like the printout, change the program.

So, for yourself, what is it time to release and let go of? What old negative belief system is ready for the dustbin? What old parental script? What old attitude and ways of making yourself wrong? 'Run a business? You couldn't run a temperature!' Imagine how that sort of feeling, dragged around behind you for 20 or 30 years would get in the way. It's time to sever the chain.

Take another few moments to write down, 'The belief I used to have about myself was . . .' and then note down the most positive statement that counters it. For instance, you could say, 'I used to believe I'm a slob' and counter it with 'I am an agent of planetary transformation'. If it's not hard to say then we're not there yet. But there's plenty of time. Rome wasn't built in a day. We're not going to become enlightened, Christ-filled beings just by snapping our fingers. Notice that even that last sentence is a negative belief system, and if you nodded agreement with it find a way of stating that last sentence more positively. For instance, 'I am an enlightened, Christ-filled being'.

What does any of this have to do with turning up at the office tomorrow morning at 9 o'clock? Just in case it's not obvious, what use is a slob whose idea of success is making a cup of coffee without spilling it, in an office whose vision potentially is transformation? The more slobs there are in that office, the more distant the prospect of transformation becomes. Are you a slob or an agent of change?

Reading about it, thinking about it, even looking seriously at it will achieve a certain amount. However, change does require some effort on your part, so use the table below to state the resolutions you will now make. State the major change you want to see and notice the commitment statement as you pass on to write a positive statement that will counter the old negative core belief that used to hold you back. Then write down three things you are doing to make this change happen for you. Sign it and date it, and know that the process is already under way.

RESOLUTION

The major change I intend is . . . [state it as happening]

I am totally committed to this and am allowing it to happen effortlessly, naturally and without resistance.

Affirmation that counters the old negative core belief:

The things I am doing to make this happen are:

1. _____

_____

2. _____

_____

3. _____

_____

Signed: _____ Date: _____

INTERLUDE

A run for your money

One day last summer I went for a run, and realised some things about abundance. You can start a run anywhere. Wherever you are is a good place to start a run. Somewhere you're not can seem a better place to run, but that doesn't tend to help you get running. If there is somewhere better to run, it would be a good idea to go there. But if that's not immediately practical, then you might as well run where you are for the time being. It's good practice for running somewhere else, and is never wasted energy.

Wherever you start your run, there is an abundance of possibilities. You can go in any direction, for as far as you like and there are few limitations that cannot be overcome. All it takes is willingness and recognition of your freedom of choice. If you focus on the limitations, that is your malady and you probably won't run very far, if at all. Initially it makes sense not to take on all the limitations at once, but to stick to what is possible. Running across a field with a bull in it, and notices saying 'Private Property. Keep Out. Foot-and-Mouth Hazard'; cutting through security fencing and electric cables to get into an area; dodging traffic on the M 25; running faster than your legs will carry you, in the dark, with your eyes shut . . . these are all good ways of proving that running is a dangerous mistake! Later on, if it still seems important to do any of these things, there's probably a way of doing them.

I started running five years ago. I'd been meaning to do it for years, but was always too busy with something else, or found some excuse. My best excuse was that it took too long. I wanted a quick fix, something really strenuous and energetic where I could feel I'd *done* something after 5 or 10 minutes. That was my attraction to judo – a sport so strenuous that a normal contest lasts just three minutes. I never really had the strength or stamina for it, and in my 20s and 30s I tended to injure myself whenever I went back to it . . . after recovering from a previous injury! I began to realise then that I needed some other activity to keep myself in shape. And I'm only beginning to realise now that if I had done more running, I'd have developed more stamina and strength, especially in my legs, and the natural co-ordination to make a better job of judo and avoid the injuries.

Some things are really basic to life, and running (or at least a serious amount of walking) is one of them. It prepares you for the short, sharp bursts of energy that may be required of you . . . about six times a day! Otherwise these demands can prove too much and it's a constant self-defeating struggle to keep up.

Running takes practice. When I started running again, after several years of inactivity, it was all rather embarrassing. I ran a quarter of a mile, and collapsed in a heap behind a convenient tree. This process of quick dash and wheezing recovery continued until an ankle gave way and I limped home. Not a very glorious start. This thing clearly called for a rethink. Result — short, 10-minute runs round the block, so home was never too far away, and I could will or cajole myself to the next corner knowing there wasn't much more to endure!

Gradually I found I could run quicker and further, and the runs began to last almost as long as the shower and change afterwards. There was also some sense of achievement and well being about this. I was not dead yet, and I was even going to give the grim reaper a run for his money. Life did indeed begin at 40, I felt.

As my running improved, a whole new spectrum of possibilities and mistakes opened up! The biggest mistake was believing that I should start each run as fast as possible, on the basis I wouldn't be able to run as fast later on. What I was actually doing was limiting the distance I could run and the lessons I could learn, but even so there were rewards. I could now run all the way (well, *most* of the way) round Wimbledon Common, about five miles in an hour or so; I could see twice as much of the Common as I could if I set aside an hour for walking.

At this point, an experienced marathon runner from Greece came briefly into my life. I had acquired enough stamina to benefit from expert assistance. We could go for a run without my disgracing myself totally or holding her back unduly. Off we set, and I was *leading*! 'You're going too fast,' she said. 'Some marathon runner you are,' I thought as I slowed down! 'The first mile you need to run yourself in gently, concentrating on getting yourself together,' she explained. 'Once you've done that, you can gradually increase your stride and your speed and keep it up much longer.' I learnt a lot that day – to place my feet in a straight line, to land on the outside of the front of each foot, to bring my feet up straight behind me, to drop my shoulders, to vary my pace – sometimes sprinting, sometimes jogging, now a long stride, now short, even walking and just focusing on breathing and posture. I'd already learnt from *The Zen of Running* how to find a breathing pattern that worked for me (three breaths out to two in, for me), to lean forward slightly, pick my knees up and float or bounce rather than push, and to do no more than was a delight in that moment. When the last run was a delight, the next one was more likely to be looked forward to. And every run produced a lesson here or a small improvement there. Did you know, for example, that the best way to run up a hill is with quick, short steps, increased oxygen intake and looking no more than three steps ahead?

My competitive mind still calculated average speed and wanted to run a bit further, a bit faster and was impatient for progress. This had its good side in that my will was given exercise too, but in the end this proved my downfall. I'd entered a 6-mile race and completed it in a very creditable 41 minutes; now my ego was keen for more, and my improved ability fed it. There had been a glorious day when I ran 6½ miles, and felt 'I could do that again!' and I just went on and ran 13 miles. It was a bit too much but I made it, and already I had a movie running in my head about entering the London Marathon and being cheered on by thousands of admirers! The next step would be a half marathon round Burnham Beeches in August 1988. I'd been running about 25 miles a week, and regularly turning in 7½ miles in an hour. So I was ready. I ran the Burnham Beeches half marathon in 1 hour 54 minutes (about 7 miles an hour) . . . and totally wrecked both my knees because

I was not used to running on roads. For the next three years I hardly ran at all and, gradually, 'running' The Breakthrough Centre encroached more and more on my time, and I got out of practice. I found I needed more sleep, and it did me less and less good. Getting up in the morning became more and more difficult, and by the evening I would be exhausted.

So, on the third anniversary of my half marathon débâcle, I resolved to get back into practice. Gradually it's all come back, and I can again enjoy the exercise and let my mind freewheel for an hour or so. I still have some way to go. Initially, I walked about a third of the distance, and I still only ran 5 or 6 miles. When I ran my 7½-mile run through the woods and up Califer Hill overlooking the Findhorn Bay, I only walked about a mile, and came back in 85 minutes. However, I enjoyed the process and the time was less important. There is a long stretch of straight road near the end of the run, uphill for about a mile. My mind dreaded it, but I closed my eyes and ran it without effort, just checking my direction every 25 paces. Running blind is extraordinary. Uphill becomes level ground, and my pace seemed to take little account of it. What the mind thought was impossible, my imagination made easy. I'll be off for another run tomorrow, clarifying my thoughts, sifting out negativity, improving my running . . . and practising abundance.

Abundance, like running, may take time. It certainly takes practice. There are apparent, usually mental as well as physical, limitations to be overcome, and the biggest of these is the needy ego. As you become more familiar with the feeling of abundance, you move into new dimensions where teachers become available to you, from whom you could not have learnt before, because you could not keep up. Then abundance takes over and you can go with the flow. After about six miles of running, it's common for another level of energy to take over. The endorphins flow and you experience what's known as 'runner's high'. Abundance is exactly the same, and it happens regardless of environment.

More haste, less speed

The most unlikely lesson for me in running has been to discover the absolute truth of the old adage 'More haste, less speed'. Running fast at the start limits the distance you can run *and* the overall speed at which you run it. Biting off more than you can chew can put you out of the race altogether. When I ran 13 miles at 7 miles an hour on roads, I overcooked it and now, 3½ years later, I can only run 6½ miles at 6 miles an hour. Learning to feel good about this and recognise the abundance even in less has been a major lesson in enjoying a short run as much as a long one, enjoying it for what it is, not for what it might be a step towards and not adversely comparing my performance now with my achievement, my 'result', at Burnham Beeches.

Success is not just running a long way at high speed. Success is being running. And abundance in running is beyond ideas of success. You estimate what you are capable of, and do half that so you can enjoy it and feel there is more where that came from. Abundance is taking what you need right now, and not necessarily the whole pot. If you run the pot dry, you risk losing everything because you have insisted on having it all *now*. Don't overdo it, especially when you're training. Pushing it to the limit is the work of the Ego. You may win a short-run result, but ongoing abundance eludes you. Abundance is a gentle sufficiency, not a bust-a-gut excess.

> **The discomfort of undergoing change is nothing compared to the pain of resisting it.**

6

---•---

Creating an Abundant Reality

W<small>E</small> each of us create our own environment. Now before you stop reading, groan or explode, let me make clear I'm going to qualify what I have just said in several ways in the course of this chapter.

A STRAIGHT CHOICE

We are responsible for everything that happens in our lives – the people, the books, the groups we get into, the business or working environment around us, all our thoughts and feelings, what we get and what we don't get. If I try to evade my responsibility by telling myself that I was worrying about such and such, then I must also take responsibility for such and such having happened and for choosing to worry about it and for hanging on to all the negative feelings instead of applying some positive energy. And I have a straight choice – I can stay miserable all day or I can choose to look at the context of my misery and see what it has to tell me and take appropriate action. I can also choose to let my miserable feelings go and have a joyful day. It's all entirely up to me.

I can no longer blame anything that goes wrong for me on somebody or something else. I can't blame the circumstances of my birth, anything my parents did, any unhappy experiences at school, antagonistic authority figures or uncooperative bank managers. By the same token I can take 100 per cent credit for everything that happens in my life too. I can take all the credit for my success and for allowing into my life the people who helped me to that success (because we chose to!), and when I am surrounded by wonderful people, I can take the credit for that as well.

How do you react to this? Does it sound selfish or arrogant? Does it sound like the most utter balderdash? Does it 'make you angry'? Can you take responsibility for the feelings you have about it or are you going to try and dump them on me?

If you don't accept the idea that you are responsible for the environment you create, you are saying you are a victim of circumstances, that someone or something else is running your life, that you have no control over it, or your feelings about it and that there is really no hope for you. I don't actually believe that for a minute, because the sort of person who gets to Chapter 6 in a book like this is saying to me, 'I've had enough of allowing other people to push me around, to tell me what to think and feel and generally make my life a misery. I am beginning to recognise that the only person who can do anything about my life is me, and I'm not prepared to dump the responsibility for that on anybody else any longer.'

SELF-FULLNESS

Those who are not prepared to take responsibility for their own lives call such behaviour 'selfish'. In the English language there is no word to describe the positive midway point between selfish and selfless. And the English language is a dynamic thing, so here is a new word for you – self-full! I encourage you to be self-full. I give you permission to give yourself permission to be self-full! Self-full people are no burden to anybody, nobody has to carry their problems around for them, they do that for them-selves, and whereas selfish people never do anything for any-body, self-full people are constantly doing things for other people, because they choose to, not because they feel blackmailed into it, or pressurised by some social convention; they do it because they want to, because they choose to. They don't look for any thanks or gratitude, that's not why they are doing it. I repeat, they do it because they choose to. If they get no thanks and if perhaps they feel aggrieved or affronted about that, they take responsibility for feeling aggrieved and affronted. It is, in the jargon, their 'stuff', not the other person's 'stuff'. They recognise that their motivation for doing what they did for the other person was not without ego; they recognise that in themselves, acknowledge it, forgive themselves and move on.

Self-fullness might be described as a sort of enlightened selfishness; you get what you want and you ensure everyone else gets what they want, without you feeling that you have to do it all for them. Self-fullness stops at the end of anyone else's nose: selfishness doesn't. It is up to others what they do with their lives, what they get and what they choose not to get. A very common reaction to this — my own included from time to time — is 'Choose this? The hell I did!', but if you didn't choose this, who did and why did they have a choice that you didn't have? The answer presumably, is because they chose to have a choice, so why didn't you choose to have a choice?

The story of Bill and Ben

Let's take two examples. Bill is unemployed and angry. It's all the fault of 'that idiot in Downing Street, the government, the wicked, fascist bosses, the capital monopolists who hoard all the money and keep it for themselves'. He feels there ought to be jobs for everyone, regardless of ability, experience, qualification, preparedness to turn up in the morning or put in a day's work. He is resentful and angry as he shuffles along in the queue at the unemployment office for his minimum subsistence dole money. He watches a lot of television, which tends to make him even more angry. He spends more and more time down at the pub, moaning about how rotten everything is. He does occasionally apply for jobs, but he never really expects to get one, and so he doesn't.

It may well be that his unemployment is the fault of

government, business and union policies, but where does that get him? Does it get him into feeling happy and fulfilled? Does it get him a job? Of course not! Only when Bill takes responsibility for the situation he is in and chooses to change it is there any hope at all.

Ben is also unemployed. Initially he was devastated, depressed and felt badly hurt by what had happened. He was a conscientious worker and gave good value. What hurt most was that other people in the same company who didn't have as much to offer were kept on, while his position was made redundant. So he sat at home and sulked for a bit, and then, in moments of great honesty, recognised that he was enjoying the break. It was a rest that he deserved. And he recognised that the only person who was going to get him out of his present situation was himself. If he got stuck in and reviewed his skills, brought them up to date, developed them and added further skills that linked his existing skills into a more cohesive and attractive package, he stood a better chance of finding work again.

As he started to take charge of his life he got more and more excited about it and talked to people about what he was doing and what he had in mind, and how determined he was to make it. He applied for 75 jobs and was turned down for every single one of them. Each time he experienced disappointment, and each time he managed to be honest with himself and look at why he hadn't got the job, what more he could have done, what the employer was looking for. Soon he got to the point of asking employers, politely and without edge, why he hadn't got a particular job, what he had to do in order to qualify for that job or some other job. He also asked who else might be interested in giving him work. The more he took charge of his destiny, the more his spirits rose and countered the inevitable disappointments of job searching.

Which of these two would you employ? Bill, who has given up on himself and is resigned to being one of life's losers, or Ben, who is using the same situation as an opportunity to learn and grow?

There is no guarantee that Ben will get a job. He will, however, emerge from the experience larger than when he entered it. Bill, on the other hand, can only go downhill. Even if he gets a job his festering resentment remains unresolved. Things are going to keep going wrong for him, because that is the only reality he chooses to see.

Positive people attract positive energy to them. People feel like doing things for them. They like being around their energy and they feel comfortable about recommending them to other people. Negative people go around with a great black cloud hanging over them and everyone runs for cover. Everyone, that is, except all the other miserable people, who feel more comfortable with misery than success and happiness. Misery loves company!

Nobody is to blame

It is, of course, very hard to say to someone who is unemployed that they are responsible for being unemployed. Not that it is their fault, or that they are to blame, since nobody is at fault and nobody is to blame, but we are all responsible. It's very hard and it's also the kindest thing to say because to endorse their negativity and confirm their belief that they are the victim of external circumstances and that there is no hope, unless those external circumstances change, is even less helpful. What one actually does in this situation, of course, is not to add to their distress by dumping this idea on them and then shrugging them off. Knowing that only if they take responsibility and change will you be able to help them or they be able to help themselves, you ask them questions and engage in discussion with a view to helping them arrive at a point where they can take at least some responsibility and move forward at least some distance.

Swimming the Atlantic

Some environments are easier to create than others. Some changes and choices are easier to make than others. I can disprove the theory that I create my own reality very easily by choosing to swim the Atlantic Ocean, without taking any swimming lessons, without preparing any support or back-up, without being in any way realistic about what I am choosing to take on. Many, even most, people seek to evade their responsibility by giving themselves impossible tasks. Having sunk like a stone 20 yards outside Southampton Harbour, they say, 'There you are, I told you so, I can't do it'. Choosing to swim the Atlantic does not mean you can opt out of taking the consequences for your choice. You are responsible for the consequences just as much as you are responsible for the choices you make, and when the things you choose to do don't work out you are just as responsible for that unsatisfactory consequence as you are responsible when you heave yourself out of the water in New York Harbour.

When you take responsibility for the direction of your life or some particular project you have set your heart on, there will usually be things to learn, things to take account of and quite often a whole series of steps that lead up to the eventual achievement of the aim you have chosen. It may well take time. Some boundaries and limitations are harder and take longer to shift than others. A good test of how realistic your choices are and how quickly you are likely to achieve them is how many other humans have achieved the same thing. As far as I know, no human being has ever swum across the Atlantic Ocean. This would be a first, and you would do well to ask yourself why nobody else has ever managed to achieve what you are setting out to achieve.

So recognise that if the aims you are choosing involve breaking through a physical boundary that nobody or hardly anybody has ever broken through before, it may take time, and if you are disappointed by failing to swim the Atlantic, run 100 metres in less than 8 seconds or live to be 500 years old, recognise that the disappointment you experience is the reality you set out to create. Most people, however, manage to hold down a job and generate the basic income they need for survival, so this is a less stretching objective. This is not to say that it may not still take a great deal of time and energy on your part.

The four-minute mile

Boundaries and limitations can be pushed back and overcome. For centuries it was believed that a human being could not run a mile in under four minutes. Then, one unprepossessing day in Oxford, Roger Bannister did it — only by a fraction, but he did it — and in some strange way he removed the barrier for others. No sooner had the 4-minute-mile barrier been broken than any number of other runners also recorded times under 4 minutes, and now, 35 years later, the world record for the mile is some 15 seconds under the 4-minute barrier. This is a nice, workable analogy. You make choices for your own life, recognise what the barriers, boundaries and limitations are, both for humanity in general and for yourself in particular. How have others overcome those barriers? What training, learning and preparation did they find necessary? Perhaps you can break through the boundary without any of that preparation, perhaps not.

Reviewing the situation in this way gives you a shrewd idea what you are taking on, how likely you are to succeed and how much time it may take. Setting a goal that results in your disappointment is just one of the choices you make; you don't get out of responsibility that easily!

THE CULTURAL CONTEXT

One of the obvious limitations or boundaries to overcome is the social or cultural context within which you operate. There is a range of possibility within each cultural context. It is, for instance, at the superficial level of making money, easier to accumulate 1 million dollars in the United States than it is to do this in Ethiopia or Bangladesh. It can still be done, it may just take longer and it may be a realistic possibility for fewer people. The boundary here is as much the result of group consciousness as anything else. If the whole group consciousness that surrounds you is against what you want to create it may take longer to get there, but once you have shown that the limitation imposed by group consciousness can be broken, like the four-minute-mile barrier, you have changed the group consciousness, you have opened up a new possibility. You can choose to do that, you can choose to go somewhere where the group consciousness is different, or access a new consciousness through books and tapes. You can also choose to leave the group; it may be more or less difficult, depending on how many others around you are opting for change, but the choice is still there and it is still yours.

Taking responsibility

While it is possible to go beyond the boundaries, most of us are more concerned with working towards the boundaries first. So, wherever we find ourselves, in whatever culture, one of the things to look at in being realistic about the aims we choose is to be clear what the range of possibility is right now. In the West the range of possibility is between having £5 per day to cover everything, and accumulating hundreds of millions of pounds in personal assets. If I have £35 per week, it is realistic to think in terms of doubling that. If I have £1 million in assets, it is realistic to think in terms of doubling that.

At the same time, in Ethiopia, the range of possibility is between starving to death in a matter of days and having barely enough to survive. The extent to which it is realistic for me to look at improving my situation there is more in terms of surviving one more day or having one day a month when I almost stop feeling hungry. There is absolutely no question in my mind but that this is grossly unjust and yet it is not the *fault* of the developed nations with their imperialistic policies. It is not the *fault* of the Third World refusing to continue its subsidising of the West. It is not even the responsibility of governments to resolve this, it is my responsibility. I am personally responsible for the hunger in Ethiopia, the destruction of the rainforests, the success of my business, for everything I do about these responsibilities, and the consequences of what I do or do not do. I, like you, must look at my life and decide what the priorities are; how I can have the biggest impact on what I care about most passionately.

I can't do it all — or at least not all at the same time! It would be unrealistic for me to say that I can solve all the world's problems by next Tuesday as well as helping Granny move house. The *reductio ad absurdum* argument never disproved anything. It merely pointed out the realistic limitations and degree of difficulty. What I have absolute control over is how I am, how I feel, what I think in whatever context or situation I (choose to) find myself.

We all know of multi-millionaires who are utterly miserable and terrified that their money will run out. Equally, we know of people who don't have two brass farthings to rub together, but who have a powerfully positive outlook on life and also seem to get by. If I choose to make £20 million because I think that will make me happy and in practice I find that it doesn't, I must immediately accept responsibility. I created the £20 million and I created the lack of joy and the fear that surrounds it. I have a choice whether to create another £20 million and see if that does the trick, or find some other way to go about being more joyful — by entering abundance, for instance.

YOU CHOSE THIS

We always get what we put out for or a lesson to learn about what we put out for, so the situation we are in is something that we have created. Now we have a choice: whether we learn from that or go on making the same mistake over and over again. People who believe that money is the answer to everything tend to keep on making the mistake of thinking that more money will be a better answer to the increasingly miserable and fearful existence they create for themselves. The situation you are in now is the result of choices you made in the past. *You have a choice whether you continue to reinforce your old belief systems or question them, or experiment with new belief systems.*

We do have a choice whether we buy into the prevailing social order and burden ourselves with six kids or a large mortgage, or heavy financial commitments or a particular type of job. We are responsible for the consequences of buying into the social order, quite as much as for opting out of the social order. You are in the situation you are in now, relative to those around you, because of choices you made in the past.

You now have a further choice – continue to believe that this is rubbish and take the consequences of that, or choose to experiment with a different set of beliefs and take the consequences for that. Either way you will be creating your own environment, because part of the environment you create is whether you feel you have a choice or not. Until you make the choice the environment you create will be superficial and unrewarding.

I have been at pains to avoid the over-simplistic presentation this idea of creating your own reality commonly receives. To distance us further from the spiritual fascism that uses all this as an excuse for insensitivity and condescension, there are four further qualifications to stress. They do not remove responsibility. They do, however, clarify what we are responsible for.

1. Others create too

At the same time as we are creating our reality, everyone else is also creating *their* reality and this will interact with and may cut across ours. It has, for instance, taken years for those who are concerned about the environment to get their point of view taken seriously by a political, economic and social system that worships growth at any price and accumulation over sensible distribution. Now, at least, our leaders are learning to use the language of environmentalism, and in due course their actions may become consistent with their words. Meanwhile the environmentalists' attempts to create their own reality in Brazil, Queensland, Ethiopia and indeed, across the planet, have been hampered and delayed.

None of this destroys the argument that we create our reality – if anything it confirms it. And it may take time. It certainly does not justify anyone in not continuing to make the effort to create a long-term sustainable reality for all of us.

2. *Responsibility for relationship*

Secondly, whatever happens when we set out to create a nobler reality, in whatever circumstances we find ourselves, we are not justified in abrogating our responsibility for our relationship to that reality. Whatever the facts, and however much responsibility you accept for them, you have 100 per cent control over your relationship to them. There is always a lesson in them.

3. *Accidents happen*

This brings us to the third qualification that needs to be made – that there are accidents. You can make a cake perfectly 100 times and then one day, without changing any of the ingredients or method, it comes out green and flat! (This is a real-life example!) There are completely random factors which it would be arrogant and unrealistic to dispute. We are still responsible for our relationship to them and what lessons we draw from the experience, and it has to be said that some people are more accident-prone than others. Whenever something like this crops up, it is still possible and responsible to say, 'I don't know if I caused this, and what does it have to teach me?' We can occasionally recognise that our escape mechanisms are not perfect, without making this a daily excuse for life not working out.

4. *What goes with the territory*

Finally, even when there is a 'good' reality created, it is quite possible for there to be 'bad' realities accompanying it. As the tyrannies fall in Eastern Europe, some very unpleasant forces have also been released. These are, it appears, the dynamics of the system – that 'good' comes through accompanied by other things we call 'bad', that they are all part of the same territory. Our problem with this, and with the whole field of reality creation, is that we insist on seeing things in dualistic terms – good and bad, higher and lower, spiritual and material. Instead of seeing polarities, if we see 'good' and 'bad' as just two ways of looking at the same thing, much of our difficulty with and resistance to the idea of reality creation can fall away; the 'light' is what faces the sun, the 'dark' is what is not facing the sun. To see success as pure sweetness and light is at best unrealistic.

Nobody said any of this was going to be easy, and yet it's not exactly difficult either; it may just take time. Most of the difficulty people have in coming to terms with this thinking comes from the assumption that I, you, he/she are single-cell creatures with one single set of beliefs and aims, and one single set of responses to life. To take a simple example, 'I' do not, in fact, feel angry. There is a part of me that feels angry; there is another part that feels angry about me being angry; there is another part that sympathises with the anger I feel and wishes I would express it in a less destructive way; and there is a part of me that knows that anger is counter-productive and likes to keep it under control. Sometimes you get a response from the part of me that is angry, sometimes you get a response from the part of me that controls anger; both are part of me, neither is the whole me and if you think there is something called 'me', you can get very confused when 'me' reacts differently from time to time. It is absolutely essential to recognise that all these different aspects of me have each had some impact on and input into the situation I find myself in now. Most of these parts of myself I am only dimly aware of, so I am only dimly aware of what has been at work creating the environment in which I now live. So if you still believe that you did not create your present environment it is largely because you are unaware of certain parts of yourself that have been busy creating that environment without exactly telling you.

THE MULTIPLE SELF

The psychosynthesis model developed by Assagioli (shown below) explains the relationship between the various parts that go to make up the self. Understanding this provides the context for work on integrating and aligning with the real you, your higher self. This in turn opens the door to the possibility of living to your highest potential.

Each of us has a unique and very personal way of perceiving reality, which, among other things, determines which levels of personality we have developed and which we are working on now. The way we perceive reality is greatly determined by the conclusions we have made about life, people, ourselves, God and the world, and these beliefs are stored in our subconscious. The subconscious is giving feedback to our conscious Self all the time and tends to attract situations that confirm those beliefs and fit in with the self-image those beliefs have moulded; whether, for instance, we love ourselves and others, whether we aim high or low, whether we set up success or failure, what we perceive, experience and feel.

We started drawing conclusions about life at a very early age, certainly within the first five to seven years, probably within the first five to seven days, and many would say within the first five to seven hours or minutes, or even long before birth. We learn that we don't always get what we want; we learn that some animals get angry, and we learn to give names to them and stereotype them. We learn at some point that life is not to be trusted, that our love is not always returned, that sometimes the bricks fall down and sometimes they don't, and sometimes somebody takes them away and hides them.

The conclusions we draw form patterns which become firmed up into belief systems. Anything that conflicts with those belief systems is uncomfortable. Anything that confirms them is comfortable, however uncomfortable that might be in itself. So life becomes a process of repeating the same old patterns of fear and failure, struggle and pain, because we learn and now 'know' the way life is; and we don't want to change it because if we start questioning the assumptions on which our life is based, where will it all end?

The thoughts we programme into our subconscious in these early years are the thoughts that create our environment now. I think I am going to fail, so I do. I think I am going to come second, so if there is any danger of my coming first I'll make jolly certain I trip up and come second instead.

By the age of about 28 a whole cast of sub-personalities has built up within our subconscious. We can deliver a brilliantly polished performance of any of these characters, and if anyone tried to take the part off us we would be very reluctant to let go. These characters we play are often gross distortions of ideals we only dimly perceive of love, justice, good etc., which can be found in our higher self or super-conscious. Between these two poles comes 'me' the self-conscious, ordinary waking consciousness, the part of me that is most visible to others, dragged down by the subconscious and uplifted by the super-conscious.

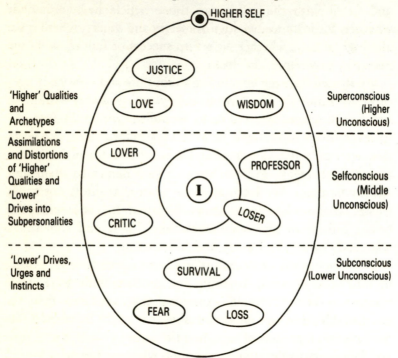

This whole conscious possibility is embraced in the Collective Unconscious

An Adaptation of Assagioli's Model of Self

Where you project attention

Where you project attention is what creates your environment. This is where your thoughts and feelings come from. This, dear reader, is your life! What you see is what you get. The perception you have of reality through the conditioning of your thoughts and feelings creates the reality you receive, and the more you apply certain thoughts, the more creative those thoughts are. What you focus on expands; where you project attention is where you are.

To take a simple example, do you remember when you set your heart on that red XR2? It was what you wanted more than anything else – a really special beast! From that point on, the world was full of red XR2s, they were everywhere, everybody had one, they were a glut on the market. There weren't nearly as many before you started looking at them; now suddenly you couldn't drive five miles without seeing one. In fact, all that had changed was the focus of your attention. There were no more of them about, you were just focusing on them, so you kept seeing them. And that's the way it is with life – we are where we project attention.

The easiest part of all this to accept is probably the idea that we create and are responsible for our attitudes to what happens and our perceptions of what is happening, in much the same way that two people look at a glass of water; one can perceive it as being half full and the other sees it as being half empty. One sees something that belongs to being full and abundant, the other sees something that belongs to being empty and a failure.

The next step, which is also not too difficult, is to acknowledge that if we constantly go around seeing things as half full rather than half empty, we will see more things that are half full and not be so aware of things that are half empty. Take this a step further. We will see abundance in our own life and in the situation around us, rather than failure. Take it a step further and you have the situation where something that most people would consider dreadful happens and you are able to see it as at least containing positive aspects. Instead of being destroyed by redundancy, which is what most people expect those in that situation to be, you are able to see the positive possibilities – the space to step back and look at what you really want to do, the opportunity to take a break and give more time to things that have been squeezed out. Instead of feeling hurt and betrayed at the departure of a long-term partner, you can take the attitude that you were complete with that relationship, it had served you well, you had learnt many useful lessons from it and it was time to move on to other contexts and lessons.

The perils of negative meditation

The final step is the recognition that having this constantly positive attitude and constantly reframing the events and situations of your life in positive terms actually creates more positive events than negative events. Seen in this way as a sequence it is only a small step from taking responsibility for your attitude to recognising that you create your reality. It is often easier for people to acknowledge the validity of this process by reflecting on how negative thoughts invariably create further negativity. You have only to think something is going to go wrong for it to go wrong. You keep seeing how it is going wrong, rather than seeing how it is going right, so you keep reinforcing and endorsing what is going wrong and undermining what is going right. The result is that, at the very least, all you see is things going wrong, which exacerbates your negative thoughts and encourages you to see even more negatively. Your increasingly negative thoughts create an increasingly negative environment, which attracts further negativity. It is quite easy to say 'NO' to someone who has said 'NO' to themselves and has NO written all over them. It is much more difficult to say 'NO' to someone who has YES written all over them and has said 'YES' to themselves. This is how whatever you think you draw to you. I like the way Paul Solomon puts it. 'Worry', he says, 'is negative meditation'. It sets your mind on a negative track and that track leads to more things to worry about, more negativity and the creation of an increasingly negative environment.

Through death to life

If negative meditation and negative thoughts have the effect of creating negative surroundings, might we concede that there is just that cubic centimetre of possibility that positive thought and positive meditation create positive surroundings? Peter Caddy, co-founder of the Findhorn Foundation, says we have wars because we are always prepared for war; once we are at peace with ourselves and prepare for peace there will be peace.

There is no question in my mind that the growing number of people who are meditating and collecting and putting out for peace are having their impact. The Berlin Wall and other events in Eastern Europe offer testimony to this, and even the Gulf crisis had an extraordinary impact for peace. Four separate navies gathered in the Gulf and the United Nations achieved greater unanimity than at any point since its foundation. We are reaching a point where each country retains a small military force for use in co-operation with all other nations to balance any back-sliding to hostility, rather than to defend themselves or bully somebody else.

Sadly, those who are at war with themselves still take their internal conflict forward. Bush celebrates a triumph for Iraq, and unbelievably for the Cold War too, while Brandt, and to some extent Heath, share their inner peace. The horrors with which we afflict ourselves, such as the endless wars and the destruction of the rainforests, are necessary because the pendulum has to swing so far one way to raise mass awareness, generate demand for change on a massive scale, and bring the pendulum back the other way. The same goes for famines, floods and other natural disasters. A major disaster on our planet often has to occur before we can goad ourselves into doing something about it, changing our consciousness, our belief system, our thoughts and the reality they are creating.

You can do this with your life as well, if you like. Just keep carrying on until things get into a real mess, and then – and only then – start taking action to turn it round. Alternatively, you can be more perceptive to the signs that your way of thinking is not serving you and make changes earlier on. The key is simply that, at any time you decide that you don't like the output, you can always change the programme.

We create our reality, abundant or otherwise, only in the sense that we have control over where we are directing our *consciousness* at this moment. Our perception of a situation decides the nature of that situation for us. This may coincide with others' perceptions which will reinforce their and our perception. This becomes, if it is not so already, the cultural norm. When I have a different perception from the norm, it may well be perceived by others to be abnormal, divisive or ridiculous. And it is only such new perceptions that contain the possibility of change.

My new perception probably involves a decision to reframe a situation — see it another way — choose to re-evaluate and change an old belief system and set in motion a new cycle of experience. As I do this I begin to have an impact on others and change not only their perception, but gradually the collective perception and therefore the cultural norm as well.

It all starts with me, or you, or the next person. It starts when somebody takes responsibility and risks being different.

The collective consciousness of humanity does not currently believe in abundance. It invests in scarcity and sees only shortage. And it is constantly surprised to find that this is its reality: there is never enough and things are getting worse. If you believe in scarcity, scarcity is all you can create. If you believe you can defy scarcity and accumulate for yourself a symbolic prosperity, you create a world divided against itself, a world of 'haves and have nots', where 20 per cent of the people control 80 per cent of the resources.

If you trust and believe in abundance, you set in motion a process whereby your needs are met and resources are available to you in proportion to the scale your work and life requires. This, then, permeates the world and the people around you. Whatever your beliefs, there is an apprenticeship to match. People go to great lengths to reinforce their beliefs in scarcity: they practise hard and become expert. Abundance has a training programme too. It's *much* more fun!

The diagram opposite shows what it looks like to shift from old beliefs that hold you back, to new beliefs that empower you.

Your current experience is created from old beliefs that create your current perceptions of the way the world is for you. And your current experience reinforces your old beliefs unless you choose to reframe them and see them in a new light.

Once you question your assumptions and give a new frame of reference to your experience, you can start to re-evaluate your old beliefs and to choose new beliefs to take their place.

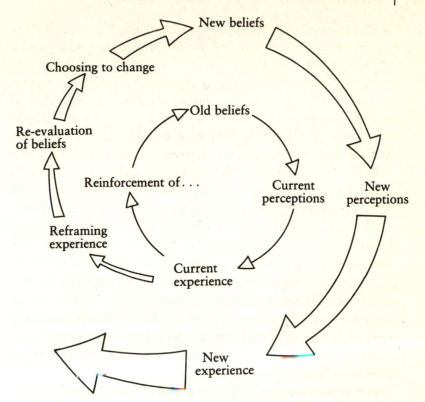

New beliefs give you a new perception of the world and your experience of life changes. You have created a new reality.

We create our reality only in the sense that we control where we direct our consciousness.

7

The Quality of Abundance

IT is time to change gear now. We have been looking at the distortion of abundance, at the mess society is in because of its obsession with this distortion, at how money has displaced the sense or feeling of abundance, at the antics of prosperity consciousness and how, in its attempt to rediscover the essence of abundance, it has uncovered only a new layer of our distorted obsession with money. And we have looked at what else gets in the way of our entering the Age of Abundance – the resistance, the old belief systems, the collective reality we continue to defend.

It is not essential to experience all this, and as members of a society that applies considerable pressure to conform, it is not unlikely that you have had at least some experience of non-abundance. Whatever your experience, there will have been lessons, realisations, moments of determination not to have it that way any more. You have created change in your reality one way or another. And you may well be looking to create further changes, even a completely new reality. This is a highly significant step forward, an important stage in the process of becoming yourself.

ALLOWING ABUNDANCE

As you work through the process of creating a new reality for yourself, that new reality gradually reveals to you that 'creating' is not quite the right word. It is more true to see yourself *manifesting* something that was always there: you cannot 'create' something that is there already! This process has more to do with letting go of a pseudo-reality than creating something new.

Even manifestation may be too strong a word. It suggests activity, whereas the process we are engaged in is more truly one of *allowing*. We will be 'allowing' the quality of abundance to come through: and the 'activity' is largely around overcoming our resistance at various levels.

Instead of seeing creativity as a process of merely attracting things (as in prosperity consciousness), we can move through seeing it as a manifestation of a new pattern of reality and grow into a place of simply *being* abundant. This involves the evolution of a deeper consciousness. Whether you call it creating, manifesting or growing, this is what is happening. You are releasing the potential energy of abundance from within yourself and finding a new way to *be*.

SEVEN LEVELS OF QUALITY

The quality of abundance has seven components. Each component represents a different type of energy, a different way of expressing your being. These energies draw in differing degrees on the three basic characteristics of humans. We think, we feel and we do. Some of us do at the expense of feeling. Some of us integrate thought and feeling well, but never do anything with our insights. And some of us achieve a more wholesome balance of all three characteristics.

This search for wholeness is at the core of the new consciousness movement. When people talk about holistic enterprise, this is what they mean, that the approach takes account of *all* aspects of human energy and its interrelationship with everything else.

Entering abundance crucially involves becoming whole, because both these expressions are ways of defining 'being'. The process of entering abundance can start anywhere. Wherever you're at right now is a good place to start. Whichever of these levels appeals to you most is where you're working and focusing attention. This is where you might start the journey into abundance. Gradually you can colonise all the other levels and then you will find you have come home.

Once you have familiarised yourself with each of the seven levels, you will find that they form a natural sequence to work through in manifesting abundance in all aspects of your life. We will look at them in that sequence now.

1. Alignment and vision

The more I identify my true Self, aligned with the Divinity, value my Self without complacency and see myself as integral with the whole, the more my needs are met. Everything else is a step on the way to this altered state of being, in harmony with natural law.

It is important to distinguish this true Inner Self, something that travels in the physical, emotional, cognitive self which is merely a vehicle for it, from the Outer Self which is a projection of that vehicle. We have to let go of the demands of the Outer Self and rise above them in order to come to a place inside where something deeply significant exists.

The Outer Self lives in the realm of Ego, personality, subject to social and cultural conditioning which reinforces the belief systems that deflect us from feeling abundant. The Inner Self lives in a place of peace and uses the outer realm to test and challenge itself. The Inner Self is our connection with something other, a cosmic force that is honoured in all religions as Divinity, but which predates and is greater than the limitations placed on it by religious definitions.

We attempt to comprehend what is essentially incomprehensible by giving it names. Bringing it down to our level of comprehension only enables us to comprehend it at our level. Our feeble definitions become yet another barrier to understanding. The natural law, metaphysics, 'beyond physics', beyond language and any institutionalised concept remains largely a mystery.

The danger is that in applying the conscious, logical, analytical mind to the less conscious, divine aspect of ourselves we make it disappear (as we do when we aim the energy of a microscope at a sub-atomic particle). We should not expect logic to be able to explain natural law. We can only reach it by rising above mere logic. The nearest we have come to this is meditation. I would call it transcendental meditation if this had not itself been institutionalised. Nobody, no institution or religion, owns this connection with natural law. And each of us can make the connection when we stop looking outside ourselves and let go of distractions that owe more to outer Ego power than to Inner Self power. (This paragraph was written two months before the launch of the Natural Law party in the UK.)

When I value my Outer Self I am in danger of being complacent. When I value my Inner Self I am in no danger, and my Outer Self acquires value from the only place it can, which is inside. One manifestation of this inner valuing coming through to the outer is that all my (outer) needs are met. Inner valuing creates in me a clear channel through which the cosmic, divine energy of all there is may flow through.

If this language is difficult to comprehend, it is because language is the wrong medium to use in approaching natural law. Alignment primarily involves being. The Outer Self has difficulty with this, because the Outer Self and its fellow travellers Ego, Personality and Outer Power in all its forms only understand doing and having. How in the Age of Abundance we integrate our two worlds of being and doing is the theme of Chapter 8. For now it is enough to be clear that we must align with the divine self and seek to connect with vision.

Vision must be distinguished from goals, targets, results and even purposes. These have their place, but only when vision is clear. The vision describes the why behind the purpose. Vision is what we are here for, the reason why our Inner Self has taken on this outer form, the contribution we have come here to make, the lesson we have come to learn. Much of humanity is deeply sceptical of this. That is its problem. There is nothing to prove that doubt is more real than what is doubted. We have a choice. We can doubt there is anything more to life than self-aggrandisement or we can believe there is a deeper purpose and see the outer world in that context.

Scepticism has made an unimaginable mess of the outer world and must now be deeply suspect itself. This, by the laws of outer world logic itself, must militate in favour of being sceptical about scepticism and looking for another way. Abundance presents itself for consideration! Oscar Wilde said that a cynic is someone who knows the price of everything and the value of nothing. Vision is rooted in values. Surely scepticism and everything that degrades and disempowers the Inner Self that connects us to natural divine law has had its day.

Abundance starts with alignment to vision.

2. Attunement and intuition

Attunement starts in the act of alignment with vision and the divine. The first step is to attune to the centre of your being. You recognise your oneness with God and your interconnectedness with all of life. This is a meditative process. Take the time and space to relax and let go of thoughts, feelings and attachments, and take yourself to the centre of your being, the part of you that knows all, knows your right place and is clear what you need. From there expand your consciousness to take in the needs of all of life. Expand this to include the whole universe and be clear how your needs can be accommodated within all the needs of the cosmos. In this way you become part of a collaborative, co-operative effort, rather than in competition for limited resources. If you are out of tune all your efforts to manifest resources will be an effort, you will be forcing the pace, pushing the river, but once you are in tune feeling good about yourself, without complacency, feeling worthy and deserving rather than low in self-esteem, viewing the world in a positive light, you are in the right space to move on to step two.

The whole of this book up to this point has been guiding you to a place of right attunement from where everything else can flow simply and smoothly. This is 80 per cent of the work and because this seems such a huge shift, such a time-consuming effort, most people prefer to get on with something else, to be doing. It is very much a case of the tortoise and the hare; the hare sets off at a great pace, busily doing, while the tortoise moves much more slowly and steadily; the hare is deflected from its course before the race is over, whereas the tortoise keeps steadily moving forward. Tortoises have had a pretty bad press and there is something very tempting and attractive about being a hare. It's all a matter of whether you choose speed and short-term result or a long, slow start and a lasting result.

The problems we face in life all start from the lack of connectedness with self; this must constantly be reaffirmed as each new challenge arises. Changing the realities of your relationships is achieved through the same process and starts with this choice of a positive reality for yourself; otherwise relationships can often become simply a way of opting out of responsibility for yourself. If you are unclear what to visualise, ask to be shown. If you are unclear about your vision, check it out in this space of openness, trust and peace at your centre. This will ensure that what you intend is whole and not just the expression of your selfish personality – the Ego, the lower order of the mind, the cravings of your animal nature. If you are not sure if your vision is right, or whether the message you're getting is from the still small voice within you . . . you may be certain it's not right yet. You will also get good indications from the support the Universe gives you . . . or withholds!

The still small voice
Distinguishing between the voice of your intuition, the still small voice within, and the noisy demands of Ego and personality is a matter of practice. Initially you are bound to confuse the two occasionally, but don't let this be an excuse for not acting on your intuition. When you feel an inner prompting, follow it instantly. The Universe will provide, so long as you are in the right space, heading in the right direction. Gradually you will learn to distinguish what is right for you and you will not only do it, you will become it.

To find your vision, to check that you are in the right space, to obtain explanation of why the vision appears to be blocked, to identify next steps, to come to terms with difficulties and disappointments, to rally others round you, the answer is always to 'turn within'. This was the entire message of Krishnamurti and yet many who followed him most ardently never actually got the message. They looked for a god, a guru, a master outside themselves, when all the time they were carrying these things round within them.

We are all being asked to experience the birth of the Christ energy within, and this does not have to happen in grandiose schemes and palatial, exquisite surroundings. Like the original birth, it can happen in the most humble and mundane of circumstances. Oak trees start with acorns. Your task in your own particular field is to hold the vision and bring it into form and manifest it. Once you are clear about the vision it is possible to move to the next step, gathering consensus for the vision, which is as good a definition of the activity of a life's work as I can imagine. Commitment to your vision involves staying with it and not moving on to something else until you are complete with this stage.

How meditation helps

We don't all have to become monks, but we do need to learn to connect with our Inner Selves. Meditation and affirmation are the main techniques for this, for working through this process of changing the reality of self, environment and relationships. Work then involves following the guidance received, catching yourself letting patterns from the past creep back in, and also catching yourself getting it right and affirming yourself.

Meditation simply requires that you be still, go within and listen. Your Higher Self, your soul, has the answers, knows what it's all about and has clarity of purpose. Above all, this part of you loves every part of you and everything there is, because this part of you is one with all there is and loves all. Engage in a dialogue with your Higher Self. Visualise your ideal self and look for your next steps to making your life more the way you want it to be. So often in life, we shift away from the original direction, get drawn into backwaters and side alleys, investing time and energy in lower priorities. Tapping back into the ideal self and its vision for us reconnects us with where we are meant to be and releases the problems we are experiencing by releasing the distractions into which we have allowed ourselves to slip. Seek answers to problems. Review your progress and priorities. Gain a wider, deeper, broader perspective. Dedicate yourself to service. Invoke the spirit of healing to be present wherever there is pain. And give thanks.

All this can take time. Just take it one step at a time and deal with whatever presents itself from moment to moment. If in doubt, ask to be shown. What do I need to focus on? How do I need to see this differently? What is the lesson in this? How can I relieve the pain? What is my next step? The path you are setting out on is the journey of a lifetime. It deserves ten minutes of your time every day.

3. Intention and pattern

In the calm meditative state you have reached focus on what you seek to manifest and give form to. Name it.

Clarifying your intentions is the third component of the quality of abundance. There are five things to be aware of first.

- Be clear what is needed and who this person is who has the need, and how you and it fit together in the whole environment in which you operate.
- Be really specific about it and get a clear visual picture in your imagination of your current situation, and your situation once you have manifested this particular thing or situation.
- Be passionate about it, not half-hearted and only half serious.
- Be positive, without allowing this to be the sort of frenzied hype that denies the self and suppresses what your unconscious is trying to tell you.
- Be yourself and be clear who that is and what that is. Ensure what *you* are asking for is what you really want and not just what your social conditioning or your anxiety about being one of the lads, or in with the girls, requires.

All this requires returning constantly to vision to clarify *why* you want what you say you intend.

Is this money or object or whatever really required by your true Inner Self, or is it merely to gratify your personality Ego needs? Manifestation can continue to work even in meeting Ego needs if you still have lessons to learn about the irrelevance and superficiality of these needs. Just watch the pattern such manifestation creates. The Ego is attached to the idea of a fast, expensive car; your Inner Self decides you need to learn some lessons, so you get your fast, expensive car. This introduces all sorts of new worry, anxiety and danger into your life. Will it get stolen? Will people with even lower self-esteem gouge scratches along it? Will the police always be on your tail, waiting for you to exceed the speed limit?

Whatever you seek to manifest it is vital to get back to the essence of what is wanted. What is the pattern? What does, for instance, a car or a large house mean in your life? What are the pros and cons? What is it you are really seeking and are there other better ways of doing it, achieving the essence in a better way, with fewer unpleasant side-effects? All this is an expansion of the fundamental premise of manifestation, which is to *be*. So you are looking at your being and your needs, at the pattern of your life and how manifesting something new in it will change your being and your pattern, what it will do for you. As Merlin keeps saying at the more dramatic moments in *The Mists of Avalon*, 'Be careful what you pray for, for you will surely get it'. You may think you are putting out for a fast, expensive car. What you may *get* is a lot of vain people who are impressed with such things, cluttering up your life.

Clear intention gives form to the abstract vision and the less solid quality of attuned intuition. It is the world of structure, organisation, planning and having an overview of how things happen. This is a more familiar world, a state in which we have often become stuck. The plan can become a straitjacket if we hanker after security, or if there is no vision but only Ego behind the plan.

Once this quality of clear intention is made the servant of vision, it is a powerful and simple tool. Clear intention, combined with awareness of the patterns and tapestry of life, puts us in charge of our lives.

4. Commitment and energy

Energy follows form. Once the vision takes form, it is possible for energy to flow through it. And once there is form there is something to commit *to*.

The right energy is a combination of commitment and detachment. You have absolutely clear specific intention, are passionately and energetically committed to it *and* at the same time you are not attached to it in any obsessive, addictive way. There is a detachment which recognises the grace of God, that is attuned to those elements of life that cannot be pinned down, that act independently of any individual human will. The right energy is definitely not the same as pushing for all you are worth. It is attuned and in right relationship with cosmic forces.

There is an experiment that serves to prove this point. The experiment relates to the effects of prayer on growing beans! One pot of beans received the right basic treatment, but no prayer, and grew to a certain height. Praying for a specific result that the beans grow as high as possible had an effect. They grew higher. However, 'non-directively' praying that 'the highest good become', that 'Thy Will be done' achieved *three to four times* the effect of that achieved through directive prayer. The beans grew to three or four times the height of those that were asked to grow tall. There is no conflict here with the principle of right intention and absolute clarity. It was necessary in both cases to be clear what result one intended, the difference was in the degree of trust exhibited in putting out for the result. Right energy means committing oneself to a particular course of action after proper attunement and then releasing it, letting go and 'letting God'.

Breaking commitments

If you start to lose your way, break your commitments, start doubting whether the way this week is going is the best, then your plan isn't working and the vision needs to be reviewed, re-energised and restated.

At any one time we have several different *sorts* of commitments, different feelings about them and about breaking them. There is a pecking order of commitments. So far from breach of commitment always being a sign of inadequacy and 'lack of commitment', it can often be a sign that our *real* commitments are assuming the priority they deserve.

Now before you conclude that you can tell everybody in your life one thing and then do the opposite, leaving a trail of disappointment, mess and frustration in your wake, let me qualify that remark! What for me makes the withdrawal from commitment acceptable is if your energy has been transferred to an even higher, more inspiring level. If something comes up that is going to take you an even more significant step towards the realisation of your inner vision, what then is your commitment? To do what you're committed to, and deny your inner vision? Or to follow your dream and regretfully let go of the previous commitment? There really should be no contest should there?

Some people avoid this issue by never making any commitments, so that they never have to break any. This is no answer, because the lack of commitment withdraws energy too. Until one is committed there is hesitancy, always ineffectiveness, but the moment one definitely commits oneself, then Providence moves too. Without commitment nothing happens. Commitment is necessary to allow luck into your life. Just don't drive luck away again by being over-prescriptive about the result.

Some useful questions emerge from all of this. Ask yourself the following.

- Do you make enough commitments to action?
- Do you, by and large, keep your commitments? Or do you often cancel, let people down, break commitments?
- When you don't stick to a commitment, why don't you and what does this say about you, your planning, your chances of realising your vision?
- When you don't keep a commitment, what thought or feeling, if any, do you have about other people involved? Do you beat yourself up, or do you go to the other extreme and totally ignore their feelings? What does *this* say about you?

- Do you make big commitments or little commitments?
- Do you commit to vision or oughts or low-level priorities?
- Do you make decisions and commitments quickly and change them slowly – or vice versa?

Okay, so you have clear vision and 100 per cent commitment to it. You make decisions quickly and change them (or withdraw from commitments) only after careful thought.

The conflict of care and commitment

The issue that needs raising next is that of care, which is inextricably interwoven with commitment. What we commit to is by and large what we care about. And yet there can be conflict.

When a commitment is broken, we are expressing care for one thing over another. We have a responsibility to exhibit care for those who may be affected by our breach of commitment – not to leave them in the lurch, or undermine a group's energy by withdrawing. This is why *any* breaking of commitment should always be seriously questioned. The choices we make are not just between doing this or that, they usually affect others and when they do, the effect on others is such a major consideration that we should only break commitments when others will support the decision totally and feel empowered by our action.

So the only commitments that should be broken are those where others involved will, if they are reasonable, support us – where the care for each other is mutual. We give adequate warning; we allow time and space for discussion, confrontation and explanation; and we demonstrate that we have weighed things up and taken all factors into account. If others cannot support us or resent our withdrawal, we should question our level of commitment not just to others, but also to ourselves. Not caring for others is a way of not caring for ourselves either, because other people are partly or wholly a mirror for ourselves.

It can be that our desire to break a commitment indicates that something is not right for everyone else too. Raising the issue with the group can result in a better solution for everyone – but just opting out denies that possibility.

The element of care for each other also interacts with commitment in one other important way. Indeed, this is where some of the biggest difficulties in commitment arise. As well as the commitments we make to our personal visions, there are commitments to people we care for – partners, parents, children, significant others, groups we join for a time or more permanently. And the personal vision can often pull one way, while the other people in our lives pull in another direction. How do we reconcile this potential conflict?

Again there are some important questions to answer.

- Who are the people who are so important that their welfare and/or my involvement with them are, to all intents and purposes, part of my vision?
- What are the situations in which their needs take precedence over my own? (Or mine over theirs?)
- Do any one person's needs frequently take precedence over my own?
- Is it their own commitment to themselves that puts me in a position of withdrawing from commitment to myself, my vision or others? Or is it their lack of commitment to self that distracts me?
- How do I feel about this? If resentful, what do I need to do?
- What is my responsibility to others when I 'let them down'?

Relationship or rubbish tip?

In many of the situations where people require you to break your commitments (to self, vision, plan or others), there will be little difficulty deciding what to do.

Your child has pneumonia – you drop everything else to be with them. But if it's the fifth raised temperature this month and these fevers arrive with the same monotonous regularity as PE lessons, that's different.

If, once in a blue moon, your partner requires your total and urgent attention for a serious discussion and this time it conflicts with a commitment to an important meeting, reschedule the meeting. But if the demands on your time are constant, the subject is always your inadequacies rather than their feelings and if their demand always seems to be timed to conflict with major growth advances for you, then it is fair to ask (first yourself, then them) whether they have made any commitment to themselves and their growth, or whether they are using you as a rubbish tip.

You need only feel a commitment to those who have made a commitment to themselves and to you. The best way to help and care for someone who is backsliding on making a commitment to themselves (and you) is to face them with what you perceive to be happening, and offer support, proportionate to what is realistic, given your other commitments.

As Carl Rogers puts it, 'Relationship is commitment to the other's growth and your own'. The primary contribution we can each make to our relationships is our commitment to our own growth. If we are not growing, we have nothing to bring to the party. 'Being' includes 'growing', since what we're growing towards is a state of 'intense being'. This does not mean we have to bring anything more than ourselves 'to the party', just that it is our whole developing and evolving, and in this moment, whole and perfect self that we bring. And this takes commitment. There is only relationship when there is commitment, care and growth, or at least willingness to grow in both parties.

The answer is not to make fewer, smaller, later, last-minute commitments. The answer is to make more, bigger, deeper, riskier commitments and keep all of them totally, unless something that represents an even bigger, deeper, riskier growth step intervenes.

Even then we still have a commitment or responsibility to care and communicate, so the energy withdrawal is mitigated. Even small breaches of commitment represent a deviation from the path of growth. When you are not 'being your word', you're not being yourself. Occasional lapses are acceptable if, as a result, you take on an even bigger commitment. Frequent lapses, however small, or failing to make commitments because you are not clear what else you might need to commit to, indicate a vital area you should look at.

Next time you're five minutes late, forget an appointment, cancel at the last minute or get conveniently sick, check out whether the reason indicates commitment or the lack of it. As we get more honest with ourselves our growth accelerates.

Seven levels of energy

In a sense all seven components of the quality of abundance are forms of energy. Your energy needs to be present in different ways throughout.

There is the divine energy with which you align to discover vision. There is then intuitive energy that runs deep as you attune to your surroundings and find your right place. The energy you put into your intention is inseparable from the intention itself. And energy is an obvious component in the three levels of abundance we have yet to look at.

The energy of commitment is the sort of energy that most closely fits the definition of the word in normal parlance. Energy means putting work into something, and tends to mean more than the purely physical work the scientific term energy originally described. There is a feeling of determination, self-assertion and passion about it. It is the energy of commitment.

Abundance requires that you maintain this high level of energy throughout the whole process, periodically reattuning to yourself and your intention and re-energising the process. Enhancing your personal energy and sense of self-esteem, doing things that give you a sense of achievement and giving yourself work to do on the lessons and feedback you are receiving are all part of this. Manifestation can appear to fail simply because your energy banks have run low.

This is the component of abundance with which you acknowledge and affirm that your power and resources are limitless because you draw on an unlimited supply. Like all the components, it can be invalidated, if the other components are ignored. Failure to recognise our responsibility to be good custodians and operate in a wholesome relationship with the planet, acting out of personal greed rather than genuine need, is a distortion of energy which then works against us.

5. Focus and mental attitude

What we focus on expands. The combination of clear intention rooted in vision, responsibly attuned and energised by commitment creates a focus like a laser beam. This is the creative process at work. When the mind is activated in this way it is positively directed.

The mind working on its own, without vision, only has the effect of getting us into trouble because it is unbalanced. The first four steps in the process of releasing abundance bring the mind to heel. And the minds knows that. So it goes to enormous lengths to interfere with the process. This is called resistance. Our most difficult task is probably to convince the mind that it can be the instrument of abundance, that it can be as active on our behalf working with abundance as it has been all these years, cautioning us against change and growth. This is the mind's task and to ignore it is to risk all. The 'positive mental attitude' that denies and tries to suppress negative beliefs is a very precarious state to be in. We have to value the questioning mind, respond to its objections and sharpen up our act so it is convinced and adds its energy to ours. Bring it to heal, rather than bring it to heel.

We just have to ensure that thinking does not get in the way. Abundance has very little to do with thinking. It has everything to do with feeling, and feeling takes many forms.

6. Relationship, timing and feeling

No man is an island and it is vital to recognise that everything else and everyone else is, in their own sweet way, manifesting as well. We live in a co-creational universe, where sometimes others are helping us manifest and sometimes we are helping others to manifest. Right relationship requires a willingness to give, as well as receive, manifestation and to recognise that, however clear your intention, there are limits to the extent to which you can alter the cosmic flow. There are times when giving is more what is required than receiving or potentialising. Right relationship is closely linked to right attunement, because you attune not just to your Inner Self, but also to your whole environment and the whole pattern of which you are a part. One of the main reasons for apparently failed manifestation is that you are out of congruence with either your current pattern or the pattern of which you are a part. Quite often a manifestation does not work out because another level of your consciousness recognises that this would be a disaster. Allow for the possibility that sometimes you really don't know what you are asking for, and a 'failed manifestation' is actually protecting you from yourself.

Right time
Right timing is also closely linked to right attunement. In fact the importance of timing runs the whole way through the process of manifestation. Quite often when a manifestation appears to fail it can just be that the timing is out, that you are out of tune with what is appropriate at this time. You may decide *what*, the Universe, the Cosmic Force has the final say on *when*.

Pay attention to your rhythms and recognise when you appear to be swimming upstream. We all know the feeling of things working out effortlessly, when we seem to be on a winning streak in a cycle of luck and abundance. Why fight it? Fighting belongs with doing, not with being and if it is not the right time, or if what you seek is extremely improbable, no amount of right intention and right action will succeed because there is not right attunement.

Against all odds
It is not impossible to have your needs met when everything and everyone else is pulling in the opposite direction and pumping energy into their needs, neglecting yours. It is not impossible and it obviously makes for a more difficult task. Your attunement, intention, action, relationship and energy will need to be that much clearer, sharper and more passionate. You will almost certainly need to take things one small step at a time. And your timing needs to be that much more carefully attuned.

There need be no cause for despair or disillusionment with

the principles of manifestation when you are really up against it and all the odds are against you. Manifesting a good square meal in the UK is of quite a different order from manifesting even a subsistence level of diet in some other places. It is not impossible, but the probability is lower and this has to be taken into account. When tremendous amounts of energy are being directed in one way you may find you're on collision course.

The overall universal pattern may require that your needs are not met or not yet, or not to the extent that you wish, if in the process others receive important feedback on their actions and what they seek to manifest or just attract into their lives. Consider the situation in any desperately impoverished area of our planet. It seems very harsh and yet at the moment it is more important that the Western world is shown clearly the effects of its avarice, greed, exploitation and manipulation, than that people are saved from starvation.

Such extremes seem to be necessary when humanity fails to heed the gentler feedback. Yes, we can have our exaggerated lifestyle and our throw-away economy, as long as we can also stomach the unnecessary murder of millions of people. As long as we fail to make the connection between our surfeit and the poverty it directly creates elsewhere we will have no joy of it and no satisfaction in it. When we take ourselves out of tune and out of relationship with the environment at large we remove ourselves from the flow of abundance it provides.

Many deprived countries are experiencing this lesson now, not just for themselves – in fact for themselves least of all – they are experiencing it on our behalf. Will we heed it or will we also need to be impoverished and exposed to famine and starvation before we get the message that ignoring the univeral laws and seeking to accumulate with no regard for the effect on others and the patterns this creates is a terminal disease?

You may be part of someone else's reality, providing a lesson for them. What matters then is how you feel about this, how you react to the situation. Only when you continue to feel loved and in tune can you maintain your journey into abundance.

Right relationship and right timing are closely connected with right feeling.

7. Custodianship and action

Once you're clear what you need and comfortable that the pattern you seek to create is an improvement, do whatever is necessary to allow the vision to manifest in form. Right action has five main ingredients: trust; action; listening; giving; and custodianship. Trust means that you ask for your needs to be met once, and once only. You don't keep harping on it, repeating it three times a day in your prayers or meditation. You ask for it once and have faith that it is working out. Manifestation has endless lessons for us in being patient, persisting and persevering against all the odds. A document circulating around the Findhorn Foundation recently contained the classic idea that 'The Laws of Manifestation are just a code name for hammers and nails!' In other words, there is nothing fancy or magical or esoteric, or even particularly spiritual about manifestation. What it comes down to is getting stuck in and doing the work, *but doing the work from the right space inside.* It's called keeping your side of the bargain with the Angel of Abundance.

This is the fundamental difference between holistic work and any other sort of work. Most people still believe that if you push hard enough you get what you want and if you are not getting what you want it is because you are not pushing hard enough. And this does work. It's the J. R. Ewing School of Philosophy, where the guy with the biggest bag of dirty tricks, back-stabbing knives and manipulative blackmail techniques wins the day. It is a school of philosophy that people are deserting in their droves.

Listening involves accepting the feedback you receive on the intention you put out. A man put out for a new partner to come into his life. He was very clear and specific about the precise dimensions of this paragon, the colour of eyes and hair, the height, the softness of voice – you get the picture. Feedback was almost instantaneous. Out came precisely what he had described from the very next doorway. All he had forgotten to specify was the sex of this new partner – so what he got was a tall, flaxen-haired, blue-eyed man. It is as well when putting out for such things to make certain exceptions, e.g. 'excluding my mother or any other member of my family!' It may well be absolutely wonderful to receive a telephone call from your mother or distant cousin in Australia, and since everything that happens in your life is right for you, who can knock it? However, you *may* have had something else in mind!

Listening includes accepting the unacceptable. You get that fast, expensive car – somebody dumps a 30-year-old wrecked XK150 at the bottom of your garden. Listening also involves responding to the call, the voice within you, instantly and this in turn means that when you put out a call to manifest something it must be more important than anything else in your life at that time, because you may well be required to take all sorts of steps to have it happen for you. You have to make time and do your bit in allowing intention to become reality. You have to do what's necessary.

The third principle of right action is the bit Napoleon Hill got absolutely spot-on when he said, 'Be a go-giver, not a go-getter'. Manifestation has very little to do with taking or even receiving. It has much more to do with giving and allowing your heart to open.

Manifestation is a learning process, so it is useful to keep a journal of your manifestation practice. Record details of what you want to manifest, the thoughts you have about the essence of what you want to manifest and the patterns you see this creating. Keep a note of any strange coincidences and how your attitude changes and finally, what results, if any, there are. You may get what you asked for. Alternatively, you may not get specifically what you asked for, but get its essence instead. Or apparently nothing happens – in which case close that particular section of the journal and a week later check what ongoing reverberations there have been which may be the lesson.

There is no such thing as a failed manifestation because there is always valuable information and feedback. You may not need what you think you need. You may not need it in that form. What you think you need may not be the best way of meeting your needs. So the way your needs are met may well come in a different form and there is valuable learning to be gained from this.

Finally, right action requires giving thanks before, during and after the process of manifestation and demonstrating gratitude by right custodianship. If you don't take care of things you are declaring your unworthiness of them and this will block the flow of abundance.

Abundance requires all seven of these qualities we have looked at to be present. Our lives are the training programme in learning to integrate their often paradoxical demands. This is no soft option. No wonder so many skip school and trivialise their lives instead.

**Right energy means committing yourself
and then letting go.**

8

Being Abundant

THE old approach to work focused on doing and having. If things weren't working out in your life, if you were not immensely successful (whatever that means), if you were unhappy with the standard of living your income allowed you, then the answer was to do more, to be more active, to put in more effort or work harder. The fundamental assumption here is that having more is what really matters. Success is generally defined in the industrial paradigm in terms of what you have, your possessions, your status and the environment you have bought. Your 'standard of living' is seen as being more important than your quality of life.

BEING SOLD DOWN THE RIVER

The whole scheme is very simple to sell. 'You want lots of money so you can have all the material goodies it buys? That means you want to be successful! You want to work your way up the ladder, where the rewards are? Then you'll have to work to get up the ladder, and what's more, you'll have to knuckle under, do it our way and whatever you do, don't rock the boat. The more you do, the more you get.' What these people are not so keen to point out is that the more you have the more you need to do to preserve what you have. Acquisitiveness is the ultimate addiction. They know, and everyone eventually finds out, that you can never have enough; there is always something more to have, to prove your success and qualify you to say 'I have a really stupendous standard of living'. Just like cigarette smoking – the cigarette you have just put out creates the physical need for at least one more cigarette. In the same way, the purchase you have just made sets you up for the next purchase you'll have to make to maintain standards, and keep yourself feeling and looking successful. It is a very attractive scam and it is never totally satisfying, which is why it is such a good scam. The preoccupation with success, material possessions and the money to obtain them distracts you from real growth for your self.

INTO BEING

Doing fixes you where you're at, at the level you're at, whereas *being* frees you up to be at whatever level you choose. If, amidst all the wasteful doing you can make room for some effective being, then you can start to be who and what you really are, rather than just a vehicle for all the things you have. You can put out the powerful energy of yourself rather than simply attracting energy in the form of money and things, so that you look like nothing so much as a magnet, cluttered up with paperclips and pins.

Whatever you want to achieve in the world of work starts with yourself. The real satisfaction comes from finding out who you are and what you can contribute, and allowing that to grow. In the process you inevitably advance because the energy of being and growth is irresistible and even more attractive than the magnet covered with paperclips. The difference is that all the energy you attract (in the form of money, things, people etc.) can be properly appreciated because there is something there to appreciate it, whereas when there is just a 'thing' that obsessively struggles to acquire and consume there is just a pile of 'things'; there isn't a real person to be seen. So this is the difference between doing a job (i.e. flogging your guts out) and really being at work. The route, as outlined in Chapter 7, is through arousing, tuning up and achieving a subtle balance of all seven levels of personal energy. This is done through training, practice and relaxation, and this is what connects you to the centre of your being. From this space what you commit yourself to, happens. And what emerges from this centred directive energy is infinitely more satisfying because it is a function of you, whereas in the industrial paradigm you are merely a function of the money and things you are addicted to.

SPIRIT IN A MATERIAL WORLD

The figure on page 152 summarises the essential differences between an approach to life that starts with the focus on being and the approach to life that starts from a preoccupation with doing.

The way of being is a spiritual way, where that word 'spiritual' simply means 'of and to do with your self – only more so'. Doing is concerned with merely surviving in the material world. Doing without being is unsatisfying, superficial, driven by a fundamental distrust of life. Being without doing, even though it is probably the ultimate and most rewarding state may be a bit advanced for most of us. What is certain is that there is no way that one can 'be' in any real sense from a state of doing. What you can do instead is 'do' from a state of being, when you will avoid the worst distortions of the material world. You are less obsessed by accumulating things to prove you exist and can keep those things in true perspective with the more important task of coming into a right relationship with yourself and your environment.

With the old laws of money, the more you *do* the better the old laws work for you. With the new rediscovered principles of abundance the more you can find it in yourself to *be* the better the new principles work.

Doing is a very grounded state concerned with the material world. On its own it can only take you into 'being active', so highly prized in industrial society. Being belongs in the spiritual

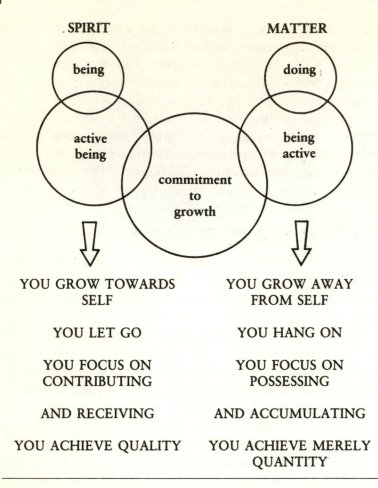

YOU GROW TOWARDS SELF — YOU GROW AWAY FROM SELF

YOU LET GO — YOU HANG ON

YOU FOCUS ON CONTRIBUTING — YOU FOCUS ON POSSESSING

AND RECEIVING — AND ACCUMULATING

YOU ACHIEVE QUALITY — YOU ACHIEVE MERELY QUANTITY

world and leads you into a state of 'active being', the original state of grace to which we are returning. What is required to integrate these two streams of existence – being and doing – is a commitment to growth, which is the turning point in so many people's lives nowadays. Without a basis in being, commitment to growth is shallow, but often once people have arrived at this turning point, they start to enter the world of being and active being. They start growing *towards* themselves, instead of growing away from self.

The secret of manifesting what we need is in being and the main principle we need to concern ourselves with is *to be*, to recognise our oneness with the divine and the all, to bring the

Christ energy into everything we do, affirming that we *have* it all already, because we *are* it all already.

WHEN ALL ELSE FAILS, BE YOURSELF

When battling your way up the corporate ladder loses its gilt, when you have accumulated a pile of assets and still feel unsatisfied, when you have tried all the ways of making yourself OK by accumulating things around you and you still need more things around you because you still don't feel OK, then you are ready to start work on 'being'.

'Being' is how you get yourself working properly. 'Being' is what the equipment was designed for. So it's hardly surprising that using the equipment for the wrong purpose, abusing it by thinking it's just a magnet for paperclips, doesn't work. It's like those signs you see in the launderette – 'When all else fails, try reading the instructions!' This is what your instructions say:

> This is a wonderful piece of equipment. Your first task is to find out what it is and find out how it works. It is very good at going off the rails and disappearing off in all sorts of directions. Your task is to take charge of it and enable it to grow. Like any toy or piece of equipment, if you force the controls or abuse it in any way it will not work very well and it will not be much fun. Please take time to find out how it works, so that you derive the maximum enjoyment from it. See you in heaven.

By comparison what we tend to do is use the fine piece of porcelain that we are as a hammer.

Everything you want to achieve in your work, whether as an employee or running your own business, or operating as a freelance, independent person, everything starts with you. If you are in the right space, connected to your Inner Self, developing and growing on all seven levels of quality we looked at in Chapter 7, then you can start to relate to other people. You can find your way through the snakes and ladders world of business. You can attract the funds and customers you need and have things happen for you with less effort, less struggle and less tension.

A higher quality of wealth

The route of being does not necessarily lead to less wealth. It tends to generate a higher *quality* of wealth and one's relationship to it is different. If I let go I can have whatever I need, whereas in the route of doing I am hanging on desperately to all the things I have accumulated, for fear they may disappear, and by and large that fear is justified. That fear creates its own reality, whereas trusting that all my needs are met creates that reality. The only difficulty in moving from the route of doing to the route of being is the fear that letting go of all that activity will lose me all the possessions I have accumulated. Many who take the plunge find their experience is quite the opposite – that when they hang on to things they are forced to let them go, and when they freely let go of things they have what they need in abundance. Along the way there are many tests, such as a large and growing overdraft to test your level of trust and degree of attachment to the material or temptations to join schemes purely for their financial gain, rather than for the benefit they may bring to the community around you, and so on.

So there are many barriers and causes for reluctance in letting go of the hyperactive doing approach. Just remember, *doing* fixes you where you are at, at the level you are at, but *being* frees you up to be at whatever level you choose and, as we said before, from this space what you commit yourself to, happens.

Attunement to self

The process of stepping into being is called 'attunement'. There are three tiny steps to take and they have a remarkable result.

- When you can find that inner space of peace and stillness and align yourself with the Higher Self, the Divinity Within . . .

- When you open your self to an honest, unconditionally loving energy and mutual support from others of like-mind . . .
- When your common purpose is in tune with the forces of nature and the plan of the Universe . . .

ALL IS POSSIBLE AND CAN BE BROUGHT INTO FORM.

The manifestation of abundance is, above all, a learning process. It is about learning how to be that presence in life that empowers and energises. All manifestation is about manifesting the sacred in our lives, ordering patterns in such a way that we are blessed and the whole is blessed. There is nothing esoteric or occult about manifestation; working for it, baking a loaf of bread, is as much manifestation as having it fall out of heaven.

Running through the seven levels of abundance can be found the two main streams of humanity – *being* and *doing*. Being is the springboard for active being, while doing sets up a state of being active. Abundance requires both streams to be combined at the point of commitment. From the side of being is drawn the power of the spirit; the side of doing is represented by the power of sex. Commitment takes both energies bonded together, as Napoleon Hill recognised (though he had rather more time for sex than spirit)!

BEYOND POLARITIES

Neither being nor doing alone has the complete answer.

- doing is concerned with attraction, trying to get the outer to come in;
- being is represented by manifestation, allowing the inner to flow out;
- 'being abundant' is about dropping the inner/outer distinction and seeing it as all one 'is' – we *have* it because we *are* it.

This adds an extra dimension to the idea that we create our own reality (Chapter 6). We need to recognise the difference it makes at what *level* of self we are creating. Is it just the Ego or personality self, seeking to create material wealth by attraction? Or is it the God-Self allowing itself to be? Or is it stuck in a rut of unreality?

The complete answer to these questions requires a number of frequently opposing strands to come together. Abundance is only real when it contains the capacity to tolerate and rise above its opposite. Abundance contains lack, as happiness contains sadness and light dark. Neither opposite has any meaning without its opposite. Sadness defines happiness and vice versa. You need a right relationship to both, an ability to slip to and fro, and live in the crack at the boundary between the two where they merge into something other, between either abundance or lack, containing both. Then light and dark are no longer at war and evil can be seen as the loyal opposition providing good with challenges to work on.

Celebrating debt

When you look at it this way, being in debt can be the best place to discover abundance! There is less confusion between abundance and money (because there isn't any). And the situation is such that you can, if you choose, separate your lack of money from your reactions to it. You can see the belief systems you have about abundance more clearly, because you are experiencing the belief systems and negative emotions you have around the apparent lack of abundance.

Do you experience fear, worry and pressure to recover the situation by paying off the debt? Does it make you work harder? Does it confirm any belief you have around life being a struggle, or your being irresponsible and living beyond your means? Do you feel you must be wrong in some way? Do you feel you're being punished? Why would you have any of those feelings?

Instead, can you look calmly at the situation and see how it serves you? Debt tends to keep us where we are. It is difficult to change direction and take risks when the debt is there as a constant reminder that there isn't enough. Is this a challenge to stick at something and is the issue commitment? Is the universe keeping you in something you need to be in because it leads to your life purpose, or is there something you need to learn? Is it an invitation to grow – and is the invitation the even bigger challenge to take the big risk, trust and go for a complete change? Only you can tell, and sometimes not even you. Then the tension is about living with uncertainty.

A question that can help here is 'If the debts were cleared, how would you be different?' If you would react by giving up work, taking more time with the family, going self-employed, telling the boss where he or she can put it, this is what part of you wants to do. And this is what part of you is resisting. This is what you need to look at, and it will also be valuable to look at the belief systems behind it. You will be in debt as long as you resist releasing the resistance. What makes debt hard is the double dose of resistance. It's the effort of resisting that makes it a hard time. Debt becomes an easier place to be when you accept it, sort out whether it is telling you to move on or hold on to something, and even feel gratitude. As long as you begrudge something (that has probably come to help you), you will be stuck with it. Accept it, learn from it and you can move on.

The Parable of Debt

External difficulties always correspond with internal blocks on self-awareness. The external debt may be a parable about something else in your life. What old 'debts' do you have on the inner? What old penalties from the past? What does your love balance sheet look like? In other words, do you have large reserves of love that are gradually depreciating, or do you keep topping them up? Do you pay up with love, or are you mean and slow to release it? Do other people resent giving you the love you feel is due to you? Or have others been giving or investing more love in you than you've been giving? Is your love balance sheet – the record of what you owe and are owed – in debt too? Debt can be seen as overflowing abundance too. It is other people investing in you. And maybe they want some 'interest'. Maybe they want more than interest, maybe they want love. Maybe you can pay off your debts with love instead of with fear and struggle.

The fear and beliefs you have around money are the fears and beliefs you have around life and love. Do you believe you can't make a lot of money and have time to be? Then it is likely you believe you can't have a lot of love and have time for yourself. What do these beliefs do for your ability to generate an income or a permanent relationship?

So-called negative situations, deprivation generally, can be very good places to learn about acceptance, self-acceptance, gratitude and therefore abundance.

Rejection is a place to learn about valuing yourself. Failure is just another name for 'still learning'. Loss gives the experience of doing without something: you might discover you didn't actually need it, or you might come to value it but in a different, less obsessive way. Loss can create whole new worlds for you, shift your priorities, take you up to your next level of development, perhaps a whole octave higher.

The question 'What do you most want to be doing?' will always have (at least) two levels of answer. One will relate to the outer contexts of life and the other to what is going on within those contexts.

At the *outer* level, one might want to be running one's own business, getting married and having children, generating a high level of income to pay for travelling, a place in the country, glorious food and a bit of grouse shooting.

Most people, I suspect, live much of their lives on the outer level, believing (as society, in the shape of parents, education, politics and other vested interests, keeps stressing) that these are the things that count. Whether they actually do count is largely a matter of opinion (framed by parents, education etc.).

The Great Lie is to believe that success with these outer level goals can create happiness or fulfilment, in any real, sustainable sense of the word.

Some contexts encourage and activate progress by being difficult, some by being easy or freeing. At some level we all choose contexts which will serve us in our progress towards growth. And as each lesson is learnt, we move on. Learning the lesson can take the form of a deep, cataclysmic experience, or merely a feeling that something which once seemed important is no longer so. A change of context on the outer is always both reflecting and facilitating a change of attitude or priorities on the inner.

The final test with any such change of context generally requires that we let go of some old feeling, belief or context. Because this old feeling or context was once very important, because we probably had a lot invested in it (financially, emotionally, whatever), letting go is usually a wrench. It involves moving from known to unknown, safe to risky, clear to uncertain, comfortable to uncomfortable, even frightening. It demands trust in ourselves and the divine process. It tests our ability to love and believe in our evolving selves. It is the stuff of life.

The challenge is not always, of course, to move on. Especially where the issue is about commitment, when the risk may be to *stay*! This adds to the confusion and uncertainty, because it removes any guarantee that moving on is always right. All we have is a best guess. All we can ever do is act on this and listen carefully to the feedback. Acting involves letting go (of the desire to stay or the temptation to move on), and letting go can be all it takes for clarity to appear about whether to stay or move on.

Happiness is a state of heart rather than mind. It is wholehearted rather than just single-minded. Fulfilment is a journey towards wholeness. And happiness and fulfilment both need a context in which they may be experienced. It hardly matters what the context is, as long as there is a space in which happiness and fulfilment can be experienced.

This process starts inside, feeding your inner power, building in you a feeling of abundance which sets the scene for happiness and fulfilment. Then, if it still matters or is necessary for some reason, there can be money and relationship.

For many people 1991/92 was a quiet space after the fierce pace of 1989 and 1990. It was a space in which to reflect on our inner relationship with our various outer contexts. Many people have been traumatised by the loss of outer identity and by their reluctance to look for inner validation. The great hope is that in letting go of the dream house, new car, private education or holiday in the Bahamas, people may discover how insignificant these things are compared with inner peace and togetherness. Affluence has not taught us to appreciate the green issues of environment and community: now perhaps depression will succeed where affluence has failed.

How strange it is that the more we have in material terms, the less we appreciate it, and the less we have, the more careful and appreciative of it we are. When did you last darn a pair of socks or appreciate a cake because it had an egg in it?!

The idea that money and affluence is the primary measure of success is a hard one to let go: it is so deeply ingrained in social thinking. Just how much is enough does depend very much on the scale of one's vision, so it is hard to put a figure on it. What is certain is that there never will be *quite* enough and there is always some further necessity (or extravagance) to reach for. At least this is true when money and power are accorded an exaggerated position in our lives, and when they are seen as the only route to fulfilment and quality of life.

What we always have to make sure we guard against is that a step forward on the outer is not a step backwards on the inner.

All you need is love

Love is both the journey and the destination. As you discover more of the potential inside you, you work more with love and work more towards love. Work is love made manifest. Work is love in action. Inner and outer.

Love is not the same as feeling or sentimentality or empathy. Feelings accompany love, they do not constitute it. Sentimentality is a form of feeling, similar to nostalgia and romance. If taken in moderation, these feelings do no harm, but they are not love.

Love involves a commitment to yourself, your evolving consciousness, your recognition of your inseparable connection with the divine whole. You cannot *not* share this with others and everything. If you make exceptions that is not love. Lovable people are easy to love. It is loving the unlovable, the Hitlers, Saddams, Pinochets, Stalins, that is the test of love. Picture someone you have difficulty loving. Keep breathing! Repeat to yourself, 'I love you. I bless you. I see the Divinity in you. I may hate what you've done, your behaviour – but I see the hurt and the essence of love in you, as in all humans.' As you release your hatred for the person, you will find your love for them, *for yourself*, for all of humanity growing.

As long as you allow fear, hatred and separation, there is no love. It is present all the time, of course: it is just not penetrating your consciousness which blots it out.

As long as fear, separation and negative consciousness prevail over love, abundance remains illusive and elusive. And as love manifests, so too does abundance.

All you need is love. Because love is all there is.

THE ABUNDANCE MEDITATION

At this point in the book it is now time to experience the abundance meditation. Find a comfortable place to sit or lie down, where your back can be completely straight, holding your hands on your knees or on the floor; palms facing upwards helps keep your back straight, and also, symbolically, opens you to receive. Loosen any tight clothing and close your eyes.

Start your meditation by breathing three or four times quite deeply into your diaphragm. Breathe in through your nose and out through your mouth. Breathe in peace and breathe out fear.

Keep breathing quite deeply and pause briefly after each in and out breath. Do this several times, until it becomes natural. Feel yourself becoming more and more relaxed and, as you move more deeply into this quiet relaxed space, focus for a moment on your physical body. Notice any aches and pains. Listen to what they may be saying and hear their message, without undue concern. Ask them where they want to go.

Relax your forehead, let go the five-bar gate. Relax the little muscles around your eyes and nose. Relax your cheeks and jaw, and let your mouth be a little open. Let go of any tension in your neck and shoulders. Imagine, if you like, a heavy cloak slipping away from your shoulders, taking all the weight off them. Feel your chest opening out in front of you and your back behind you, so that there is plenty of space inside. Let go of any tension in your solar plexus and stomach, and notice how effortlessly you breathe.

Relax your hips and buttocks, and let this feeling of peace and relaxation flow through your legs and feet, and down to your toes. Feel your arms and fingers equally relaxed. Just let everything click effortlessly into place and relax. Take as long as you need for your body to relax.

Now notice your emotions. What are you feeling? Listen to what your emotions are saying and hear their message. Then let your feelings just be. Visualise a mountain stream if you like, bubbling down the side of a mountain – sometimes dancing and leaping joyfully, sometimes slow and deep and shaded by trees. And for now, let the stream flow, let it be.

Now notice what thoughts you have. Listen to what they are saying and hear their message. Reassure them that you value their contribution and that for now you need some peace and quiet. Assure your thoughts you'll get back to them later and tell them all about it. And, if you like, visualise above the mountain stream, an almost clear blue sky, with just a few fluffy white clouds floating across it. As you watch the clouds they vaporise and disappear. And let your thoughts disappear with them, floating off into the ether.

Stay completely still and begin to notice your heart beating, in the huge dome-like space you created between your back and your chest, and feel the quality of unconditional love flowing from this central heart-space to fill your entire body. Know that your heart loves you unconditionally, and without reserve, and know that this is the source of your abundance. Acknowledge the abundance of your breathing, your heart-beat, your access to unconditional love. Take some time to allow this feeling of unconditional love and abundance to flow out from you into your home and place of work, out into the community, the country where you live, and allow it to spread out from there to all the other countries and oceans of the world. See the whole globe of earth glowing with abundance and go as far out into the universe as you wish, recognising the abundance of all there is. Take as long as you need to feel your connection with the abundance of all there is.

Now bring yourself gently back through the Universe; see the earth again, glittering like a diamond in the sky. Feel into what the earth needs and see its needs being met with grace. Tune into the environment closer to your home and into what is needed there, and see those needs being met. Now connect with your own needs and see the abundance of the Universe coming to serve them with unconditional love. Know that this is so. Allow your needs to present themselves to you. There is no need to think, or force the pace, or push the river. Let your needs become known to you, and know that they are being met. Make no distinction between what appears to be 'out there' and what you see inside. Feel yourself in the flow of abundance and see your world as it could be once you let go of the needy Ego and resistance. Take some time to be with that picture. Notice what and who else, if anyone, is there.

After a time, acknowledge that you are a droplet of Divinity, trusting in God and the abundance of the Universe. Now that your needs are clear and specific, put out for them, knowing as you do, that they are already met; resolving as you do to keep your side of the bargain with the Angel of Abundance. Detach yourself completely from the result and give thanks.

Know that you may always return to this space inside whenever you wish and that now it is time to take your leave. Do whatever is necessary, and gently bring yourself back to your physical level again. Feel the tips of your fingers and toes. Become aware of your breathing and open your eyes, feeling bright, alive and abundant.

Fulfilment is a journey towards wholeness.

9

Seven Steps to Abundance

IN this chapter we return to the seven-level theme of Chapter 7. There the focus was on the energetic quality of each level. Here we look at the activity required at each level, the questions to be answered. At the end of the chapter all the ideas and thinking in the book come together into an action summary, to which you can add your own resolutions.

STEP 1. FIND THE VISION

If you don't know where you're going, and you're not clear why you intend that, you're unlikely to get there. The process of entering abundance starts with clear vision, taking charge of the direction you want your life to take.

Unravelling the maze

This is likely to be a gradual process, as today's vision of the future becomes tomorrow's reality. It can be like walking through a maze. You can only see so far ahead. As you turn each corner you have a new perspective and a new range of possibilities opens up. But you have to *go* to the next corner. Wherever you are is a good place to start. The things you have been doing, the strengths and talents you have developed, the people and resources you have gathered around you, are a good indication of where your priorities lie at the moment. Even if you are not too happy about your present position, this is fine as a starting point.

Those characteristics that contribute to vision are probably the ones you enjoy. Ask yourself these questions.

- What are the activities you have most enjoyed in the last 10 years?
- What do you remember from your earlier life that was really fun?
- What do you most want to be doing for the next 10 years?
- Which of your strengths and talents are a joy to you?
- What do people keep telling you you're good at?
- What is special about the *way* you do things?
- What is the quality you express?
- What do you feel is new and exciting about you, just emerging?
- Who are the people you love to be around?
- What do you treasure?

Review your answers and divide them into two new lists, as shown on page 166. As new thoughts and feelings occur to you, add them to the lists and keep selecting until you have 10 things in each list.

One list is of things you ideally want to be doing, e.g. training acrobats, making corn-dollies, eating ice-cream, talking to people on the phone, playing chess, planning a holiday, visiting new places, running your own business.

The other list describes how, ideally, you want to be, e.g. spontaneous, relaxed, meditative, sexually active, warm, sociable, open-minded, organised, transforming, unpressured, exhilarated.

Which list is easier to write? Which do you have most difficulty reducing to 10 qualities/activities? What does that say to you? Would you like to live only in ideal doing, or only in ideal being? What would you lose if you had to choose?

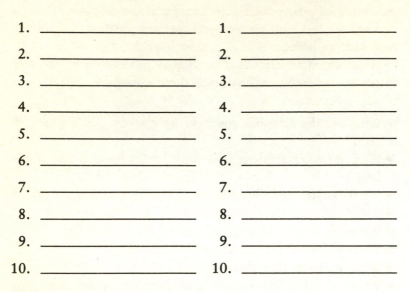

IDEAL DOING

1. _____
2. _____
3. _____
4. _____
5. _____
6. _____
7. _____
8. _____
9. _____
10. _____

IDEAL BEING

1. _____
2. _____
3. _____
4. _____
5. _____
6. _____
7. _____
8. _____
9. _____
10. _____

Which list makes your heart sing? Which items give you a glow? Go back over the lists and put a star against the items you care deeply about, two stars if you care passionately about them. Then select from each list the single thing you care most about and put a circle around it.

What if the thing you care most about in all the world is not *on* either of your lists? Consider why this has not penetrated your being or your doing. If you cared about transforming the planet, you'd be doing something about it and exhibiting the quality of transformation in your being. Whether it is clearly present in your list or not, affirm it now. You then have three important elements of your vision.

Ideal doing _____

Ideal being _____

Most care about _____

Keep asking WHY?

Take each of these three ingredients in turn and ask WHY?

- Why is this my ideal activity?

- Why is this my ideal way of being?
- Why do I care about this more than anything else?

And keep on asking WHY until you get to the bottom of it. Doing this with a friend, or having two chairs to sit in, one where you ask yourself 'WHY?' and one where you answer, can be an enormous help.

Notice where you get angry or emotional. You're coming closer to truth. The ideals you've selected may not be your ideals at all: most people don't live their own vision, not before the age of 40 anyway. Anger is a sign that at some level you do not believe your own PR. Tears can be a sign you are touching into a level of vision of which you have lost sight.

The nearest we usually get to vision is the identification of goals, purpose and focus on results. Vision is different. It is the WHY behind all these things, that makes the whole journey an inspiration instead of just the arrival. There's a smile when you start, not just when you finish.

Money and vision

It is natural in our money-absorbed society to have financial goals, and lists of things you want to buy. What is all the money *for*? What are all the things you want to buy with it? WHY? Why do you need these things? What are the material things and status symbols *for*? Why do you feel you need a pile of money? There's nothing necessarily wrong with it, as long as you're clear why. Some visions require larger amounts of resources than others. Anita Roddick's Body Shop vision is global and transformational. It has kept expanding its impact over the years. Each new arrival point opens up new levels of possibility. And the money flows in to support the vision in proportion to the needs of the vision.

Getting clear what the money is for tells you about vision. And that can now be your focus.

Uncluttering vision

Encapsulate your vision in about 10 words. To do this draw on your ideal doing and being, what you most care about, what you do for a living and what emerged from answering the question 'why?' e.g. running imaginative training programmes in a holistic way for green, ethical, self-employed people.

Does it involve other people in any way? In the end it is sure to involve hundreds, even millions of people, but at this stage we need to be sure the vision does not depend on other people's involvement. Too many people live their lives in other people's pockets.

What is inspiring about the vision, independent of the enjoyment you get from other people's reactions to or involvement in it? I would have to adjust my vision statement to read, 'Working in an imaginative, holistic, green, ethical way to transform my world'.

Now we have to remove everything to do with process and activity. Vision is the most rewarding basis for action, and at this stage we need to be clear what in essence is the quality of the vision, even when nothing is happening. The essence of my vision is 'Transformation through imagination'.

Take another example. Your vision might be all about DIY and helping others take care of their homes. Serving customers and doing what's necessary to keep a shop going is your idea of heaven. Without people and process, you might discover that the vision is about 'craft excellence in a home environment'. Going deeper and more abstract might reveal that the underlying vision is Beauty, and that this is what informs everything you do and every relationship you have. Think of the impact this vision would have on places like Texas Homecare!

Envisioning

The best place to find your vision is inside. Then you work with the vision outside. The quality you work with is imagination, creating a powerful idea which reflects your values, passions and strengths. It must inspire you, so that it inspires and enthuses others.

Every day, start by creating a quiet space where you can relax and let go of tension. Consciously relax each part of your body in turn. Attune (tune in) to that part of you that just knows what's best, your 'centre', 'wise being', 'true self', or 'higher self': it is your divine telephone!

Take a few slow, deep breaths, filling your diaphragm, and ask yourself . . .

- What do I most want to be doing? Why?
- What do I most care about? Why?
- What is a significant step I can take to be more with this vision?

OR, if you like, instead of posing questions, imagine a situation at work or anywhere the way you want it to be and as if it already is. Listen to what comes up and record it, together with any resolutions. This is your priority – do it first thing every day.

Express/share your vision with others who are prepared to share theirs. Don't tell everyone, just a few people close to you. The way you are will communicate your vision and energy to others.

Ensure your vision/intention includes giving, sharing, serving, as well as receiving, listening, hearing, being open to let go and transform.

Take time at least once a month to review how your priorities are changing, and where there is a conflict. Clarify what you want now and where the conflicts come from – internally, past conditioning and externally, how your vision is not integrated with the vision of those around you. Once you are clear where the conflict arises, you can resolve to let it go or use creative visualisation to see it changed.

Finally, review which of the seven steps you are working on, how to tune up those you underdo and bring into balance those you overdo.

- Too much fantasising about vision, or imagination on a back-burner?
- Too much meditation and fine-tuning, or life cruelly out of balance?

- Endlessly planning and directing events, or bobbing about like a cork in the water?
- Becoming autocratic, or never standing up for yourself?
- Fidgeting about details or blithely ignoring them?
- Living in an emotional maelstrom or being cold, distant and uncommunicative?
- Dashing about exhausting yourself or staying in bed all day?

See the whole picture

Sir George Trevelyan says, 'Always ignore the demands of the Ego and choose the course that leads to the maximum wholeness whatever'. See the whole picture, how your purposes both for giving and receiving affect not only yourself, but also everything around you, and ensure that these purposes are for the very best and that you can commit yourself to them wholeheartedly – for anything done wholeheartedly and with the divine spiritual quality of love is perfection.

In addition to asking questions of yourself in meditation, it is also very powerful to use this quiet space to visualise what you intend. You could also imagine the place you work as you want it to be; hold the picture in your mind's eye, and see what it looks and feels like, and how people are with it in detail. Allow it to shine and glow, and attract people and resources to it effortlessly, and know that this is an absolute reality, easily within your grasp. When you do this write down or draw the picture of your ideal workplace as you visualise it. Then you can return to asking what steps you can take to be more with this vision.

These two techniques of meditation and creative visualisation fit together perfectly and are vital strands in the new approach we are exploring. Having resolved on your purposes and some sensible next steps, take responsibility for them and set about achieving them. Every day, make certain the first thing you do is part of this new process and do it until it is done. As you move forward return to the quiet space to sharpen the vision, remove any blocks and resistance you experience, and keep moving forward. Defining vision is an iterative process. As the vision becomes clearer it also becomes clearer how you can give it form, which in turn makes it easier to make commitments, which in turn assures fulfilment. But be careful. Only ask for what you *really* want, because you will surely get it!

STEP 2. DEFINE YOUR NICHE

Alignment with vision takes you flowing into a closer attunement with yourself and your surroundings. We are working here with the practical application of the seven qualities of abundance we looked at in Chapter 7. As we proceed, the steps to take become more solid and grounded. It all starts in the abstract realm of vision (Step 1). Next, we shift into the realm of intuition, which helps you to be sensitive to the signs of the times, your environment, trends and needs in the world around you. It ensures that the direction you give to your work provides a perfect match between you and your environment. What is your special niche? What are the trends that will support you? What is that gap in the market that is yours, and yours alone, specially created by the powers that be for your benefit? The work you do must fit you like a glove. It should draw on your unique personality, your special skills, as well as your vision and hopes, and it should be in tune with the world you move in. Developing your vision is also discovered in the process of finding your niche, that unexploited, unsatisfied corner of the market place that cries out for what you alone can give. Find yourself, find your niche, find your fit, then you can find your feet.

Enjoy yourself!

Your search for abundance must embrace the novel concept of enjoying yourself. Get clear what would be more fun than anything else you can think of. Then think who will pay you to enjoy yourself! Instead of getting paid for being miserable, working hard and living in perpetual fear of being sacked, be open to the possibility of a benefactor to fund your dream.

Who *will* pay for you to have fun?

Who is crying out for what you have to offer?

If you think there is nothing special about you, you haven't even started looking. Go back to the beginning of this chapter and really work with the questions this time. Ask other people how they see you and listen, especially to those who are most enthusiastic and fulsome in their praise of you.

How do you want to work?

Reflect where you want to work, with whom, in what sort of company. Research what kinds of skills those places are desperate to find and take responsibility for becoming what they want. Realise your uniqueness and raise yourself above the crowd. Be yourself. Be different.

Look at how this world you want to enter operates – where it congregates or comes together, who influences opinions, how they do things at the moment. Draw up a tightly defined picture of your ideal, desired environment. Don't just draw on your left (analytical) brain. Intuition means learning from within, looking to the right (intuitive) brain. Its voice is quiet and insistent, where the Ego is loud and brash. When you get stuck, look within for a hint, an answer. And when intuition calls, follow it without question. It will never ask anything unethical of you – only Ego does that.

STEP 3. PLAN THE WORK

Notice how energy flows from one step to the next. As you define your match with your environment and nestle into your niche, the form of your life begins to be defined.

This whole chapter is about creating a plan, firming up on what you intend to offer, to whom and how. This is the content of your intention. Most plans explain in great detail *how* something is going to be done without ever making it clear *what* that something is, or *why* it is being done. This is why planning has such a bad name. However, when you have a powerful idea matched to a crying need you absolutely must plan how it will be realised.

Planning and organisation form the process whereby good ideas can be realised. Without a plan there will be endless false starts and wrong directions. Important things will be missed and progress will be slow and frustrating. A good plan reduces the possibility of loss of momentum and keeps up the impetus when the going gets tough.

And it is only a start point, constantly reacting to change. You think through the implications of your intentions in advance, and ensure that the pattern they create is both desirable and feasible. Then you position yourself to receive what you need.

Ask yourself some questions

During this planning stage, be clear about the following.

- What is the overview, broadly how it is all to work out?
- What is the pattern this creates in your life?
- How does the form and structure of your life need to change?
- What are the possibilities, the most important things to do?
- What 10 tasks, if you do them, will take you the biggest step towards where you most intend to be?
- What are the milestones along the way?

The difference between this plan and any plan you've made in the past is the integrity and ethical space you've taken up, clear of Ego and attachment.

So, your new plan will not be rigid or dead. It brings your idea to life. It involves spelling out your assumptions and intentions so that you are clear where you are going. A good plan creates flexibility and the possibility of rapid change in response to 'external' pressures. Without a plan all you have is chaos.

STEP 4. MAKE THE COMMITMENT

This is the point where you stop saying you're going to do it . . . and do it! You have drawn up the plan and taken the decision to act. Now you put in the necessary work, allocate the resources, write the cheques and in whatever way it takes, go out on a limb.

Commitment involves going past the point of no return.

> Until one is committed there is hesitancy, the chance to draw back, always ineffectiveness.
> Concerning all acts of initiative and creation there is one elementary truth the ignorance of which kills countless ideas and splendid plans: that the moment one definitely commits oneself, then Providence moves too.
> W. H. Murray, *The Scottish Himalayan Expedition*

So consider what are the commitments you will make:

- to yourself;
- to your loved ones;
- in terms of time, energy and money.

Are you prepared to stick at this, no matter what?

And will you, as you make the total commitment, release all attachment to the result? Will you find it in your heart to love yourself unconditionally?

Will you put out for your vision with love and determination?

Will you stop saying 'Yes' when you mean 'No'? Will you take full responsibility?

STEP 5. SPELL OUT THE DETAILS

This is where you draw on your powers of concentration, because once you have a clear idea what you are doing and are fully committed to it, it becomes easy to concentrate on the essential details – budgets, cash flows, control monitors, contingency plans for fast reactions to changes. So what precisely needs to be done and in what order? How are you going to go about it, step by step? What are the means to the end?

It is fatal to look at details until you are committed. If you do this all that happens is you undermine yourself. If you find this is happening, the answer is to go back a step and reaffirm your commitment. And if this is difficult, retrace your steps still further until you find some solid ground.

The mind's contribution to abundance is to work out in detail what resources you need, and keep account. You might have a plan that includes the general intention to receive £12,000 over the next 12 months. The mental detail work is to clarify when this is needed and what for. Once you have done it once it then becomes much easier to do it for subsequent years.

Question your expenditure needs

List all your major expenditure needs and question each in turn. Do you really need this or is it, like chocolate, a substitute for self-love? It is a good idea to make one estimate of your absolute minimum needs and a supplementary list of 'desirable deferrables' – things you would like, and still feel are needs, but you can defer them until later. Of course each list raises further questions. *Is* that *really* the absolute minimum? Is that a need or a luxury you could do without if you shared yourself with others? Or have you under-estimated – are you limiting yourself by not believing you deserve the resources to be you?

The exercise you do might look like the Expenditure Chart shown overleaf. The first column of figures states what you currently believe is the minimum you need. The second column states by how much you can *reduce* this; the third column shows the extra you want for desirable deferrables.

Annual Expenditure Chart

Expenditure	Current	Reducible by	Desirable deferrable
Home			
Mortgage/rent	£3600	(£900)	
Gas, electricity, oil, water	£300	(£100)	
Repairs and maintenance	£100	(£100)	+ £500
Building and contents insurance	£150	(£150)	
Television licence etc.	£100	(£100)	
Furniture and equipment (specify)	–	–	+ £750
Telephone	£200	(£200)	
Living			
Food and drink	£2000	(£1000)	+ £500
Household groceries	£50	–	
Clothes and shoes	£50	–	+ £250
Cleaning and laundry	£50	–	
Recreation			
Health care and sport	£300	(£300)	+ £250
Personal growth support	£300	(£300)	+ £500
Books, magazines, subscriptions	£50	(£50)	+ £100
Entertainments	£100	(£100)	+ £250
Eating out	–	–	+ £750
Holidays	£300	(£300)	+ £750
Travel			
Car purchase/repayments	–	–	+ £2000
Car running costs	–	–	+ £1250
Other travel	£850	(£100)	–
Financial			
Gifts and tithing	£100	(£50)	+ £1000
Money management schemes* (pensions, insurances savings)	£250	(£250)	+ £750
Taxes – poll, income, National Insurance*	£3150	(£2000)	+ £5400
Repayments not covered above	–	–	–
TOTALS	£12000	(£6000)	+ £15000

* See text opposite

The hard edge of money

Whether you are working with expenditure aims of £6,000, £12,000 or £27,000 per annum (and I've worked with all three, with a lot less and a lot more), you can struggle and feel hard done by . . . or you can feel abundant. The amount of money doesn't actually matter. It's just the context you're working with. Having more money will not solve anything. Being more abundant is the only path. Working responsibly with money is part of that path. Being prepared to take on a legion of new tasks is also part of the abundant way forward. Budgeting may be one of these tasks. Cash-flow management almost certainly is. And each of these things takes on a new meaning in the Age of Abundance.

Your personal budget becomes a statement of commitment, a measure of the resources you are prepared to invest in actualising the vision. It is the homework you need to do to clarify intention. Cash-flow forecast represents your intention translated into the most tangible terms, though the word 'forecast' may be inaccurate since not even the weather seems reliably containable within that word! Hold on to the idea of intention.

Actual cash-flow represents the energy flowing through you, again represented in simple tangible terms. It is just one marker of the energetic quality of your life.

Some of the items in your budget or cash-flow need reframing. Pensions, life insurance schemes and other savings are just names for surplus, an excess of abundance over current needs, systems of custodianship designed to cover large future expenditures. Suppose you need resources in the future to give you time to write or manage a charity project, or run for president, or to make a major purchase which will be needed for a later stage in the life of a project or a child. A pension, saving or insurance scheme is a good place to allow abundance to grow gradually over a period of five, maybe 10 or 20 years. It is wrong to think that abundance always has to be a hand-to-mouth affair. That is too much of an over-reaction to the old paradigm of accumulation and hoarding. Abundance likes you to work *with* it, and not just bale you out because you haven't done your homework.

Finally, tax is the tithe we pay, the percentage of added value that we return into the community. It is a recognition of our connectedness to our environment. The fact that in Britain, the government takes over 50 per cent out of almost every exchange without any expression of gratitude or humility is a test for each of us in loving unconditionally and forgiving.

Money is energy

What it all comes down to is that money is energy and the way it works in our lives is a reflection of the way we are.

With this in mind consider how you see money flowing through you over the next 12 months. How much comes in and when? How much goes out and when? When are you in surplus, when are you holding others' surplus for them? Notice this reframing of debt. It is not a bad place. It is actually a place of great responsibility and abundance. Others are investing in you, providing you opportunities to work with trust, ethics, self-love and humility. And there are equally important opportunities for them in it too.

STEP 6. GATHER THE TEAM

Once you get clear in yourself you can begin to gather others around you. People with vision who have done the work necessary to ground the vision are irresistible. Their energy, vitality and enthusiasm flow out.

Enthusiasm is catching; it involves other people in your idea. Develop magnificent relationships, relationships that magnify you and those with whom you have relationship. Be energetic and energise others so you may draw on their talents. Develop your network. Whom do you need to involve? How do you keep up the energy of enthusiasm? Contacts are vital and it is true that it is not what you know, but whom you know that counts. You'll be amazed how many people you know who can help you and who want to be involved, once you develop a powerful vision. Understanding what makes people tick, connecting powerfully with people at work, selling your skills, even getting money from the bank, are all about cultivating and developing contacts. This is why the focus of this book, and of the 10 years of training and workshops on which it is based, is always on the individual.

STEP 7. TAKE ACTION!

Now it's time for *activity*! Nothing can stop you! You must just be fit and active, and prepared to roll up your sleeves and get stuck in. Your idea is only an idea until you take some action and make your mark. So what's next? What will you do? What *precisely* will you do? And when will you do it? If not now, when?

Theories and plans are all very well, but it is only when they are put to work that they count for anything. Work is love in action and the first prerequisite for success is that your work is what you love more than anything else. This is especially so because it can be a long haul establishing yourself in rewarding work. It's not a 100-metre dash, it's a marathon, so it had better be what you most enjoy.

Faith in yourself

You also need faith. This word faith has been greatly misunderstood. It originally meant taking a risk, because you believe deeply in something, so it's at the essence of the new approach to work. There will be all sorts of things that you need in your work – money, equipment, people, contacts, customers, employers. Having checked that you really need something, focus calmly on it and put out for it. If you are not into praying now, you soon will be! If you are on the right track, doing the right thing, for the right reason, you will get what you put out for, your faith will be justified. It may not come in quite the form you anticipated, and it may take longer – sometimes a lot longer — than you want, but it will come if you are patient and when you are ready for it.

Meanwhile, persevere and persist in your intentions, listening attentively to what the Universe supports and what it seems to make difficult. This is the process of taking your vision through into action. Because your vision reflects what's most important to you — your idea of fun — there will be no more problems making work your highest priority, being fully present, giving your full attention to it, making the necessary commitment. What makes this approach different from any other is its focus on the individual. There are few standard answers, except in the most mundane areas of work and life. Each individual must find his or her own way. A book like this is a pathfinder. It reflects the journey of thousands before you, the possibilities and the pitfalls. It can guide you through, but it will not do it all for you. It is up to you to take responsibility for your own abundance, and for your own learning.

Your soul may have other ideas

Action is where so much of the learning happens. It is only when you act that the Universe can give you feedback. This feedback may take you faster than your controlling self is comfortable to go. It may seem to indicate a different direction, or it may be testing you. Will you resolve to listen to the feedback and keep responding?

What if, having done all this work on vision, tuning in to abundance and getting whole, your soul intervenes with other ideas? Was it really the vision of your soul, or just another level of Ego/personality? Can you then release your attachment to the vision and step closer to what your soul seeks? Working with soul, vision and abundance is no guarantee of success, especially socially acceptable, material success! If your soul needs you to get in a mess in order to learn and grow, you'll get in a mess.

The measure of success is not money, but learning and growth.

SUMMARY – THE 7 STEPS TO ABUNDANCE

The list which follows summarises the contents of this chapter and introduces a simple colour code which you can use as shorthand for describing the energy and activity of each of the seven levels. The colours may well be familiar to you as they are one of the schemes related to the chakras, the centres of human energy identified at seven points in the body in Eastern philosophy. This is a *very* old idea which has simply been given a new set of clothes.

1. VIOLET – FIND THE VISION
   Use your *imagination*. Create a powerful idea, which reflects your values, passions and abilities. It must inspire you, so it inspires and enthuses other. What *does* inspire you?

2. INDIGO – DEFINE YOUR NICHE
   Flex your *intuition*. Find your niche. Be sensitive to the signs of the times, your environment, trends and needs in the market. Be sure your idea provides a good match between your talents and the unsatisfied needs of people in the market place. What *is* your niche?

3. BLUE – PLAN THE WORK
   Draw on your *design* skills. Think through the major implications of what you're doing without getting bogged down in details. Put yourself firmly in the flow of money, ideas, influences, information and goods. See the overview. How *will* it all work?

4. GREEN – MAKE THE COMMITMENT
   Apply your *will*. Stop saying 'I'm going to do it!' and actually take the necessary steps. Allocate the necessary resources. Take some risks. Increasingly assert yourself and make space for yourself. How committed *are* you?

5. **YELLOW – SPELL OUT THE DETAILS**
   Apply your powers of *concentration*. Once you have a clear idea of what you are doing and are fully committed to it, concentrate on the essential details – cash-flows, systems, detailed budgets and contingency plans for fast reaction to changes. What *precisely* is involved?

6. **ORANGE – GATHER THE TEAM**
   Exhibit all your *vitality*. Involve other people in your idea. Develop 'magnificent relationships'. Be energetic, and energise others. Draw on their talents. Develop your network. Whom *do* you need to involve?

7. **RED – TAKE ACTION**
   Time for *activity*. Nothing can stop you now, but you must be fit and active. Be prepared to roll up your sleeves and get stuck in. Your idea is only an idea until you take some action and make your mark. What's *next*?

THE 49 STEPS

To finish this chapter and consolidate its message into a checklist for personal action, here are seven crucial actions to take at each of the seven levels. Add as many extra resolutions and actions as you wish to create your own action plan for abundance.

VISION (*Violet*)

1. Practise envisioning and being who you are daily.

2. Identify your true Inner Self, aligned with the Divinity.

3. Clarify the why behind the what of your life: if you're unclear what to visualise, ask to be shown.

4. Encapsulate your vision in 10 words, your key quality in one or two words.

5. If you don't like the printout, change the programme: if you want to change the world, first change yourself.

6. Follow your bliss: and remember your soul may have other ideas.

7. Be on a journey towards wholeness, arousing and balancing all these seven levels of energy.

NICHE (*Indigo*)

1. Set aside priority time for personal growth and inner work, with support.

2. Research the world you want to get into.

3. Make 10 lists of 10 people, influencers, friends that support you or pay you to have fun.

4. Practise distinguishing Ego and intuition: listen to intuition and act on it promptly. Always look for the lesson in the situation.

5. Look at your shadow. Let go of your addictions and outer attachments (money, security, acquisitions, a home etc.).

6. Stop worrying about money and appearances. Trust and be open to your needs being met. Receive gifts and charity joyfully. Give as you wish to receive.

7. Take life with equanimity. Take time and space to relax, meditate and look within for answers. Don't be economical with the truth, either to yourself or others.

PLAN (*Blue*)

1. Take time out regularly to take stock, review, plan and reprioritise: things may take the wrong form initially.

2. Question all assumptions and react critically to politicians and other received wisdom.

3. Name your intentions. Intend clearly and affirm the positive. Check what pattern you're creating.

4. Prioritise. Which tasks, if you do them, will take you on the most significant steps towards vision? Decide what 10 per cent of the things you might do, that you will do.

5. Identify what blocks your progress and work on it. Share the situation with a friend.

6. Do all the exercises in Chapter 5 especially pages 89 – 92, 94, 95, 96 – 7 and 100 – 3, and fill in the resolution table at the end of *this* chapter (page 187).

7. Embrace professionalism and balance it with the grace of God.

COMMITMENT (*Green*)

1. Value and love yourself unconditionally, without complacency or external validation. Open yourself to an honest, unconditionally loving energy and mutual support.

2. Take a stand. Take responsibility. Don't give your power away. Make commitments and stick to them. Only break them in favour of bigger, deeper commitments, and do it cleanly.

3. Listen to the negative voices and do it anyway. Don't suppress 'negative' feelings. Acknowledge, express, understand and come to terms with them.

4. Do the self-assessment in Chapter 2, starting on page 30.

5. Focus and detach: totally commit and release all attachment to the result. Talking about a trip is not commitment: booking the ticket is.

6. Develop a comfortable relationship with money – not possessed by it, nor self-denying. Look at your belief systems and resolve not to be owned by them.

7. Say 'No' if you feel 'No'.

DETAIL (*Yellow*)

1. Nail it all down. Detail never created anything, but lack of attention to detail destroys many ideas.

2. Decide what you really need and what is deferrable. Profile precisely.

3. Recognise that reluctance to deal with the detail is a sign of lack of commitment . . .

4. . . . But so is attention to detail at the expense of everything else. Keep it in perspective.

5. When your mind wants to interfere and won't be quiet, tell it not to worry and reassure it that you'll report back later. (Alternatively, invite it to translate the Bible into Bulgarian, while you get on with something else!)

6. Be flexible to people's circumstances. The mind at its best is flexible and comfortable with change, ambivalence and reaction to circumstances.

7. Bring your mind to heal.

PEOPLE (*Orange*)

1. Come into relationship with yourself. Then you can come into relationship with others.

2. Surround yourself with positive people to look up to and syndicate the work too.

3. Make no judgements. Blame no one (yourself included). Care for people, respect, support and value them. Give appreciation daily.

4. Enjoy yourself. Have fun. Don't defer happiness. Be happy now. Give parties.

5. Share your abundance. Tithe 10 per cent of your personal income to people and organisations you value. Be a willing party to others' manifestations.

6. Draw on support. Connect with others on the same path. Use external consultants and brainstorming groups to trigger new thinking.

7. Take pride in your work. Turn down work that disempowers you. Do no more than is a delight in that moment.

ACTION (*Red*)

1. Every day, first thing, do something that takes you a step towards vision.

2. Keep your side of the bargain with the Angel of Abundance. Do what's necessary with love, from the right space inside. Take your personal growth to work.

3. Be a good custodian. Honour what you have; reduce your consumption dramatically. Question the necessity of every purchase. Use less of everything. Buy locally-produced goods and food. Buy things that will last 30 to 50 years. Be a 'SWELL' (seeking sufficiency with elegance living lightly).

4. You can only deal with what's in front of you. Don't push to do more than you can in this moment. Work well, not hard.

5. Measure success in learning and growth. Nothing else.

6. Think big . . . start small. Start wherever you are and set off slowly. Don't overface yourself or bite off more than you can chew. Watch that Ego is not in charge. Have faith, patience, persistence and perseverance.

7. Appreciate your abundance daily, especially in hard times. Celebrate debt and flow with its message. See the opportunity, the lesson in everything. Give thanks.

   Finally, draw on this list and all the work you've done to make a clear commitment to abundance, using the format that follows.

The measure of success is not money, but learning and growing.

RESOLVING ON ABUNDANCE

The vision I have that connects me to the Universe

The crying need it meets. Who will pay?

The form I have given it (outline of the plan)

The resources I need

to start

during the next year

What I am committed to do to allow the vision and resources to come through

The patterns it will make in my life and beyond

Whom I am involving in my vision

This or something even better is my reality now. Thank you.

Signed _____ *Date* _____

10
•

Working for Yourself

THIS is a time of unprecedented change. A major transformation is under way. A great deal of preparation has been undertaken, mostly at a deeply personal level. Gradually individuals
are coming together and having a dramatic effect on the
collective. A symbol of our times is the collapse of the Berlin
Wall. Now it is time to integrate this transformation into the
part of our lives where it has been least in evidence – the world
of work.

The word 'abundance' symbolises the practical manifestations of this new approach. This is more than positive
thinking, more than prosperity consciousness, more, much
more, than the accumulation of wealth. Each of these still
affirm separation, whereas abundance affirms connection to
Universal energy.

The new abundant approach to work can be both fun and
financially rewarding.

WORKING TO GROW

Work is a place we each create in order to grow. Initially it is
a place to put into practice the skills and theoretical knowledge
acquired through education. It is a laboratory for experimenting
with our potential. We see how well we cope with the various

demands placed on us. The early challenges are about our ability to respond to instructions and discipline. Gradually we take on more responsibility and learn about working in teams. Partly because this is a new experience it is exciting, because we are learning about ourselves, growing and stepping into our potential. We have lessons to learn too about receiving, whether it be praise, appreciation, money or reprimands. These all have a heavy impact upon our sense of ourselves and on our self-esteem. Being underpaid, under-rewarded or well paid and under-appreciated can all hurt. And even being well paid can make us overly dependent on external influences; so if the job comes to an end or we are passed over for promotion, the effects can be devastating. Money starts to take control of us and we can become dependent on money to prove in some way that we are OK. But no amount of money can create abundance.

The workplace is not just somewhere to go and get money, it is clearly a place for us to work on our self-esteem. Money is just a vehicle for challenging our sense of ourselves. The point comes where we have to decide whether to continue to be slaves to the system or, and this comes to much the same thing, rebels against it, or whether we hear what is really being said, take charge, take control and take responsibility. Whether we continue to react to the lessons of the workplace at a superficial Ego level, or begin to make some real progress by reflecting what they have to tell us at a more meaningful level is a personal choice – perhaps the most important decision we ever make.

Initially this means seeing what we can *do*, then how we can be with people and strengthen our mental capacities. It then provides us with an opportunity to assert ourselves at a deep level and find our place in the order of things. Many people stop at this point, sadly because work is also the place for us to find meaning and vision – the *WHY* behind it all.

INTEGRATING WORK AND LIFE

A great many people are now asking questions about their lives and the things that seem to control them and set up barriers and cages. Most of this work on personal development, most of the growth in consciousness, has been undertaken outside of the workplace. A gulf exists between the work we do on ourselves and the sort of activity required of us in the jobs we do. We might call the work we do on ourselves 'inner work' and the jobs we do to support ourselves the 'outer work'. Very little has been done to date to bring these two worlds of work together, to integrate inner work and outer work. The inner work seems to be reserved for evenings and weekends, the outer work is what happens between 9 and 5 o'clock in the workplace. The business world has largely ignored this new questioning and the changes in attitude and consciousness that are taking place. They seem content to leave this work to others, to separate it from the 'real world' and treat it as a hobby, rather like knitting, golf or stamp collecting. They have not seen the connection between the changes taking place and the commercial priorities of business. And who can blame them? Much of the language of the new consciousness has been esoteric and inaccessible, while much of it seems overwhelmingly naïve; a point of contact has been elusive.

It is imperative to take the ideas of this new consciousness outside their normal, closeted environment and the time is now ripe. The world of work is ready, not least because there are business people who have enough sense of surety and security in themselves to look at something new, while realising that there is an urgent need for some completely new initiatives and approaches.

The world of work can benefit from integrating the new ways in which people are thinking, the new consciousness of personal growth; and we can all find in the work we do the most valuable arena for our own personal development work. We must cut through the jargon and mumbo-jumbo of both business and spiritual language, so that those in the business world and the world of work generally can see the benefits of encouraging people to empower themselves, and those working with spirit can derive the benefits that come from a more commercially grounded approach. Other books on business ignore the personal spiritual dimension; while other books on personal growth ignore the importance of work. The time has come to look at personal growth in the context of work, integrating the two, instead of seeing the conflict between people and organisation, work and life.

A PERSONAL GROWTH EXPERIENCE

The major issues in business are merely symptoms of something much deeper, reflecting the human spirit. It is important to take responsibility for our own situations. Blaming others will get us nowhere; neither will blaming ourselves. We are all responsible and the first step towards something better is acceptance of that responsibility.

Work – and especially self-employed work – is the ultimate personal growth experience. Whatever issues we have around our own value, self-esteem, our abilities, how other people see us, these issues will come up most sharply in the context of work. Put yourself in a face-to-face selling or negotiating situation, and everything you need to know about the opinion you have of yourself will be apparent. As long as everybody is pretending to be somebody else real communication and real understanding is more-or-less impossible. The main resistance to doing it is probably the fear that it might work and we will learn that we have been missing out on the simplest way to do this thing. The fear of failure, the fear that it might not work, is just an excuse. The real fear is the fear of success, the fear that it might work and we will have to cope with a much faster-moving dynamic situation.

Work engages most of us for around half our waking lives and takes up an even greater percentage of our active energy, so the main place for any serious change to take place is in the area of work. Any philosophy of life, whether suggesting a new consciousness, a closer connection with some greater or higher purpose, or just a technique for coping with stress, is of limited value if it fails to integrate the work context. There has already been a substantial shift.

Good news, bad news

Companies have responded to the basic demands of the work-force; the need for more realistically priced goods; calls for job satisfaction, more participation, protection for employees after retirement, career development and redundancy counselling. They have also responded to calls for pollution control, consumer protection, partly because of legislative measures, with something like social conscience and care for the environment. But there are still symptoms to be found of what happens when work lacks vision. We still see high staff turnover, often as high as 30 per cent every year; low morale, as indicated by absenteeism and sickness; under-achievement and disaffection. It is often difficult to establish what a company's direction is. It wants to make a profit, and it is not quite certain what for, other than to create a larger organisation with even less idea of why it wants to create profits.

Obsession with money and material things indicates that we cannot think of anything better to aim for. Strikes, disputes, lack of co-operation, demands for an even shorter working week, all indicate that people are not doing what they want, not enjoying what they are doing and not feeling that they are going anywhere. When company politics assume a disproportionate degree of interest, and an atmosphere of conflict and brooding hostility abound, it is clear that people do not feel involved at any but the most superficial level. To a large extent we have got by and just coped so far and this is no longer good enough; it is time for a major change, an acceleration.

The steps we have taken so far have been a preparation for a major shift to an all-embracing holistic approach to work and its relationship to people, the environment in which we operate and people's deepest desires. It is time to move away from the polarisation of work from the rest of life. On the one hand there are many people who accept the need for a job as the most obvious way to foot the bills, and have fun somewhere else. On the other hand, there are those who subscribe to a new approach to life and yet don't take it into the work context. In extreme cases these people opt out and maintain a position of lofty isolation. If this is also penurious, this sometimes even seems to be preferable. As an alternative some subject themselves to a daily bludgeoning by some heartless, unsympathetic organisation. This is as meaningless and frustrating as work that is undertaken without any sort of consciousness. Companies are, in most cases, only just beginning to be aware of this because few employees will admit to hating their job publicly. Criticism leads to loss of job prospects or redundancy, so fear is all that keeps people at work. It is a miracle that most organisations work at all.

Two ways out

There are two ways out. The world of work can adopt the new consciousness and acknowledge its new responsibility to provide an environment which puts people first and encourages their personal growth. And those who have discovered a higher purpose to their lives can turn their vision into reality by creating their own work, whether within organisations or outside them. The work of transformation is largely undertaken by lone pioneers, chipping away at the concrete to allow the release and growth of the individual. For organisations this work is of fundamental importance; without it they stagnate and are unable to respond to the changes necessary for their survival. There is a lot to be learnt from the new breed of self-employed owner/managers and entrepreneurial small businesses, where the integration of life, work and a new sort of consciousness is most apparent, because there are no organisational constraints or oppressive peer models and because to survive in that world you must care passionately about what you are doing. It is personal vision that keeps them going and the lack of it that explains the high failure rate.

One other place where major changes are afoot and this fundamental shift in attitudes is reflected is in the world of training, which has responded to the growing recognition of the need for a different and closer relationship between people and organisation. This, in turn, reflects the tide of concern and external pressure over corporate morality and health, as well as green issues. The whole new set of priorities in which quality of life figures prominently, and fewer concessions are acceptable, is being accommodated more readily in the world of training than in most other places. Training in the past tended to focus on providing skills and information to correct deficiencies. Its style was brash, didactic, masculine, fitting people to the needs of organisations. Now a more person-centred approach has emerged to redress the balance, and this works to the benefit of the individual as well as the organisation, because if Jane can actually be Jane instead of pretending to be someone else, there is likely to be more of Jane's energy, enthusiasm and talent present at work. Companies desperately need to attract and retain female staff at all levels, both to counter shortfalls in available labour caused by a severe drop in the numbers of young people leaving school, and to integrate the qualities women can offer, so demographics are also helping to introduce a new consciousness. Women returners and third agers (people over 50) are in demand and have the potential to counter the Essex man influence. Both women and people over 50 tend to be more mature and concerned with values and ethics, rather than just financial reward.

The business dichotomy

The fundamental point that differentiates conventional business from holistic enterprise is its attitude to money. Conventional business measures itself in terms of its success in accumulating resources, particularly money. Holistic enterprise may well be just as successful at accumulating money, but the money is purely incidental. The task is to grow and evolve in consciousness, so that one does not just *do* the business, one *is* the business – inseparable and indistinguishable. In many ways it is much quicker and easier to just do the business. I don't have to do any work on myself, or look at the shadow I would rather not acknowledge. I don't need to think about anyone else or the environment or the patterns I am creating. I can just go out there and biff people about. Cleaning up the planet afterwards is someone else's job. 'One of these do-gooding new agers can do that, and if they had half an ounce of commercial nous they'd make a fortune from it!' Doing it purely for the money does make business and life terribly straightforward. You can afford to be totally single-minded because there is only one issue – 'What will make me the biggest killing?' – and there is all that money coming in to compensate for the empty feeling inside, and all the endless hard work to do, so there need not even be awareness of the emptiness inside. It can all look very attractive, whereas the holistic practitioners can appear to be having a dreadful time of it; their poor old car is falling apart, they've only got one old television, they can't afford meat, poor dears, and they can't afford proper clothes, they have to kit themselves out at the Oxfam shop. 'It's really wonderful how cheerful they seem to be despite it all!'

The holistic approach is equally straightforward, equally simple and you can be equally single-minded about it, though whole-hearted describes it better. Whichever route you take, there will be a considerable element of effort and work; with holistic enterprise the work is more on inner levels, and with conventional business it is more on the outer levels. In both cases money will be generated, but in holistic enterprise this will be sufficient to meet your needs and will generate a sense of well-being, whereas with the route of conventional business the danger is that no amount of money will be enough and you will be left with a sense of dissatisfaction. You may be a big cheese, but you will feel cheesed off! Which route is *your* money on?

WORKING FOR YOURSELF

Wherever we work we can decide to work for ourselves, to think of ourselves as freelance and pretend we're MD of our own patch. It can be a hard and frustrating task in a conventional workplace, but it is less hard and frustrating than feeling a victim. Being a model of vision, integrity, clarity, commitment, good sense, enthusiasm and fearless activity does have an impact. It affects those around you. It makes a valuable contribution whether you're aware of it or not.

Join the few brave souls standing out against the old system, fighting the constraints on freedom of action and expression in the workplace. Culture change programmes may falter. Human resource development programmes may be closed down. You are still your own person. And it certainly helps to consider at least part-time or out-of-hours self-employment as an element in your career strategy, giving you a greater feeling of control over your work. An independent income and assured outlets for creativity and sharing are pretty much essential to personal growth.

In the end the best place to work for yourself and on yourself is in your own business − not just a scaled-down version of the old villain, but a holistic enterprise founded on the principles of love and integrity.

New recruits to self-employment talk about how wonderful it is to be 'working for a boss who loves me'. This sums up the benefits admirably. In self-employment you can work out your vision without being held back by the absence of vision in your working environment. Owner/managers have to translate this vision into a thundering good idea. As it gets more solid their confidence grows and they come to think bigger. You can drive a coach and horses through most business ideas, which is one of the main reasons why 80 per cent of new businesses fail, but with vision and imagination your idea will *be* the coach and horses. This is the basis of success, since vision is what differentiates and makes you magnetic.

The match or connection you seek to make is with customers rather than employers. Customers can be less depressing than employers, because customers are looking for neat answers, excitement, reliability, service, thrills and these are fun to provide. Employers may have a less exuberant vision and appreciate qualities that are not so much fun to deliver. They have their place, of course, often as providers of apprenticeships for budding entrepreneurs. But in self-employment you get to conspire and spend your time with like-minded people you have chosen to be around as suppliers and customers. You can't choose your family (well, you can and do, but that's another movie altogether) and you can't choose your workmates, unless you're self-employed.

When you're the boss, or working in a small co-creative enterprise, you're ideally placed to receive and react to feedback from all quarters. This guides you towards authenticity and abundance. There is no escape – you designed it, you made it, you tested it, you sold it, you set up the systems and you're the boss. The feedback is deafening, and you are supremely well placed to act on it, not least because as managing director of your own show, rather than a cog in someone else's machine, it is easier to see the grand plan.

Showing commitment

There are few better ways of working with commitment than running your own business. In business the moment of commitment is when you stop blathering and waving your arms about and put your plans down in writing. Just blasting off into something without thinking it through is not commitment. And the plan does not have to be for something massive either in order to exhibit commitment. In fact, drawing up plans for some vast project that never actually happens because it is unrealistic and goes beyond the bounds of reasonable probability is more a sign of lack of commitment than commitment. There is a very much higher degree of commitment when the plan is a step-by-step process and you are setting off to put in place the first step, which is simple and fairly readily attainable. This exhibits far more commitment because the chances of your having to do something about it are much higher. Think big . . . start small. This is the route of true commitment. Those who are only satisfied with big plans, expensive propositions, large buildings and plush carpets are working on the Ego level, not holistically. Starting small and insignificant can be a major test for sensitive Egos.

A BUSINESS PLAN

Your business plan is a clear statement of intent, the sign that you have decided who you are and where you're heading. It forces you to be immodest and spell out your specialities without succumbing to Ego. And a good plan is flexible. It recognises what can happen to 'the best-laid plans of mice and men'. It knows that 'life is what happens while you're making other plans'. It is a start point, a commitment to be your potential, rather than a straitjacket.

Writing down the plan ensures you have matched up what you're doing with the market and the wider environment. It tests the viability of your ideas, and provides a dummy-run: the plan is like running the business for a year without actually running it. In *fact*, having experienced the year in theory, you *may* be able to skip it in practice and go on to the next year, which is less certain.

You have to put your money (and time and energy) where your mouth is and provide security for investors who are often not as open to commitment and risk as you are. For yourself, as Carl Rogers has it 'the only real security is the preparedness to embrace insecurity'. It is a very fine balance – taking a risk without being irresponsible, being secure without stagnating, differentiating between acceptable insecurity, self-defeating carelessness and blinkered self-denial.

The plan is a statement of self. Implementing it is a major act of self-assertion, testing whether you can integrate money, love and power without getting too big for your boots. All the issues you have around money and self-esteem are accentuated when you have to sell yourself daily, negotiate prices that support you and raise money, basically on your own head. It is not for the squeamish.

REWRITING THE FINANCIAL TEXTBOOK

Self-employment can be undertaken with as much lack of consciousness and awareness as any other work. It can be simply about doing the work and making money. Or it can be a place to re-evaluate the aims and even the terminology of the business world. The business plan does need to contain a lot of detailed information, but a more holistic approach keeps it firmly in perspective.

Most people who attend business courses and even, sadly, many of those who run them, think know-how and information is all that matters. To be sure, without know-how you can get into serious trouble, but even the most expert knowledge of tax and systems does not make a business. *It has far more to do with vision than VAT.*

Most of the familiar business and financial terminology acquires new meaning when looked at from the holistic perspective. **Price**, for instance, is, without doubt, the most fiercely argued of all subjects, because the price you charge is so closely wrapped up with your level of self-esteem. An exaggeratedly high price can indicate low self-esteem because the Ego needs the proof of value that a high price-tag is perceived to bestow. By the same token, a price that is below the going rate indicates a distinct unease with valuing oneself, either in comparison with others or not. Price then becomes a measure of how highly you value yourself.

Our **profit and loss account** measures the service we provided and the service we received, the value others saw in us and the value we saw in them, and shows whether, on balance, the sums worked out in our favour or not. What complicates this is that the energy of giving sets up a reaction in the Universe, which ensures that we receive as much – many would say 10 times as much – as we give, so if at the end of the year we appear to have given more than we have received there may be something wrong with the quality of our giving and the energy in it. Profit is a measure of our growth – not just financial growth, but personal growth, growth in justifiable self-esteem. Profit is, after all, what we live on. It represents the amount of money we need in order to sustain ourselves. If there is no profit there is no sustenance and no growth.

Our **balance sheet** records the resources for which we are responsible and which are in our temporary custodianship. It is important to ensure that we are not accumulating unnecessarily high levels of resources, since this blocks the flow.

The **books and accounts**, similarly, represent the care we are taking of the resources in our custodianship. Not keeping the books is not taking care. Keeping your accounts in a Sainsbury's carrier bag under the bed is not very holistic either.

Capital is abundance accumulated from previous years' activities and other manifestations to finance the next stages of our growth, both financial and personal. **Return on capital** is the natural energetic reaction to application of energy. **Cash flow** is simply an expression of how you see the energy of money flowing through your business and your life. If you cannot produce a one- to two-year cash flow, you have not looked at the pattern of money in your life and you deserve the response any half-intelligent potential investor is likely to give you.

So, all the things investors and bank managers worry about are important. Not because money matters at a material level, but because it reflects the energetic quality of our lives. Dealing with the detail is also valuable as a sharpening tool for the mind. It gives it something to deal with and keeps it absolutely clear.

GROWING THE PEOPLE, GROWING THE BUSINESS

Finally, your own business is one of the two best places to learn about yourself through your personal relationships. Whatever you find difficult in your most intimate relationships is reflected in how you are at work. And in self-employment you are in relationship with so many more people for a host of reasons. The way people see you and the level of your interaction with most of them is transformed. (Some people, it has to be said, take an altogether unhealthy interest in what you're up to, though even they can be seen as helpful checks and spurs to higher endeavour. At the very least they provide more challenges for your ability to love unconditionally.)

In order to handle these relationships with others successfully, you must come into relationship with yourself. Other people provide constant material for you to work on – failure, rejection, conflict, disappointment, humiliation, bad debts and as many pleasant surprises. They are agents of universal feedback, the angels' hands and feet! Because of the close relationship of love and money, the work you do on relationships, coming to love yourself and others, is highly germane to having money flow actively for you. Because money is just a substitute for love, it is a one-way traffic – working on money does little or nothing for your love bank balance!

The key to effective sales promotion and communication is love, connecting with and integrating all of yourself. What gets in the way and stops you getting your message across is not being real, not being you, so your energy doesn't connect. The same applies to team management. Until you say 'Yes' to you, team management is not possible, but as you learn to manage yourself and be whole, you can throw away most of the books on the subject. What holds a group together is what holds any relationship together – constantly caring for each other's well-being, and your own. Because self-employment gives you such opportunities to grow and be yourself, you come into relationship with yourself, then with others, then with the wider community and so out to the planet. You will become part of the global shift from fear and conflict to love and abundance.

Small business is where this all happens, because it *has* to happen. Eighty per cent of new businesses fail within two years, but then 80 per cent of new businesses seek no support from training or other support agencies. There is a close connection between these figures. Some businesses do succeed by sheer determination, but being open to vulnerability, learning, growth, major transition and change make for a more dependable route, the path that has been described in this chapter.

It is also possible to apply this personal growth approach to work in larger companies. Indeed, over the next 25 years we can expect it to become the norm. In 1982 Sir John Harvey-Jones, Chairman of ICI, said, 'At the moment ICI UK has 66,000 employees; by the year 2015 I anticipate us employing some 3,000 full-time, plus a hell of a lot of part-timers.' Five years later 18,000 jobs had already gone, a great many of them through support for people entering self-employment and other personal growth routes. (Quoted from Francis Kinsman, *Millennium 2000*.)

If 95 per cent of ICI is to go part-time, why not the whole industrial world? And, if so, why wait 25 years to discover what large companies only seem to be able to offer when you leave them? In other words, abundance instead of just prosperity.

Work, especially self-employed work, provides a crucial reflection of who we are, how we're doing and how we're being with trust, commitment and co-creation. This is the stuff of holistic enterprise development, the focus of The Breakthrough Centre's activity which is the test bed for all the ideas in this book.

As you put the ideas here into practice, you will be wise to draw on support, connect with others on the same path, find out how they have evolved new ways of working. Working *for* yourself makes sense. Working *on* yourself makes you human. Working *by* yourself just makes you miserable. So join up with others. Become part of the holistic enterprise network. The grass *is* greener on the other side of this fence!

Work is a place we each create in order to grow.

Afterword
—•—
Working for the Planet

THE planet works hard for us. When we work with abundance, we repay the favour: we work for the planet.

The Green Movement is primarily about our relationship to each other and to ourselves. The hurt to the planet hurts us when we are in relationship with the planet: to do this we have to be in relationship with ourselves. The work we do on ourselves opens us up to awareness of and connection with our environment. As long as we are narrowly focused on our own selfish aims, nothing else impinges on our awareness. Selfishness is working for yourself without working on yourself: it keeps you in separation. Working with abundance brings you into connection.

In the Age of Abundance we find fulfilment without harming others. We meet our needs without pandering to our greed. Our search is for a good living, for sufficiency with elegance, living lightly (SWELL). We apply the wisdom that comes with years.

THE VANITY OF HUMAN WISHES

In explaining this wisdom to others we have two main problems. We have to convince those who are lining up to obtain for themselves our exaggerated Western lifestyle that it is an unattainable mirage and not worth attaining. And we have to explain why abundance is not infinite. Gandhi's famous line, that there is enough for every man's need, but not enough for every man's greed, answers both points. He further pointed out that it took all the resources of the planet to feed the British lifestyle, and there aren't enough planets to translate that lifestyle to India. Juvenal, in his satire on the vanity of human wishes, written nearly 2,000 years ago, concluded that all one should seek is *'mens sana in corpore sano'*. Nothing else has any validity.

We have had 200 years of planetary asset-stripping to create a 'high' standard of living for a tiny percentage of the world's population. We have glorified it and made wealth the only value. Now we are surprised to find that the other 99 per cent of the world wants a slice of our cake too. We will need to apologise to them for our crimes, pay the price and admit that we, the great white overlords, got it totally wrong. We have to return what we have stolen and accept a lower standard of living, because 'higher' is shallow and 'lower' is deeper. Such an act of contrition will be very good for our spiritual growth.

The trouble is that those who need to do most in this process are those who are the least well equipped to do it − the pompous bastions of outer-directed, status-symbol-driven society. This is the tragedy of the environmental movement, that it has to battle with the self-serving prejudice of those in power, so individuals in the movement can feel inadequate and disempowered at a practical, material level.

To attempt to counteract this I have striven in this book to focus on what you, and I believe anyone, can do starting today, to make an impact in your own life, trusting that it works through to the collective. Inner power will always win over outer power because the prizes of outer power have no value to the followers of inner power. Outer power doesn't understand inner power so cannot fight it. Inner power wins on the inner, and gradually colonises the outer. We must just stick at it.

Plenty to take care of

One of the arguments against the idea that this is the Age of Abundance is that abundance is 'by definition' infinite. So there is nothing to worry about and no need for us to limit our material objectives. This is the terrain of prosperity consciousness (see Chapter 4). What we have to communicate is that the limits on planetary abundance are self-imposed. When we waste what we have, when we have more than we absolutely need and are profligate, when we are poor custodians, when we are irresponsible and abuse the planet, we destroy its capacity for abundance.

In this sense, our inner work, self-awareness, responsibility, self-restraint, focus on inner values and environmental concern *create* abundance. We create it in the sense that we do not destroy its natural gift.

Obsession with outer growth is a dead end. Responsible inner growth, not harming others, not accumulating at the expense of others, allows abundance into your life. As we focus on being good planetary citizens, we add our piece to the environmental blueprint for a new, sustainable economics. If we focus on what is right for the environment, we will get economics right. It has already begun to happen.

A point of contact

The nearest we have come to finding a point of contact has been the recent growing concern with environmental matters. It is as though we as humans have been prepared to put up with being desensitised and having restrictions placed on our freedom to be real, but have drawn the line now that our life on this planet is in danger. The future of the planet is an issue both sides can understand and be engaged by, each from their own perspective. Even though most of the reaction has been superficial and some of it has been downright dishonest, the two perspectives can begin to merge. The Green Movement provides an excellent model of how the 1990s and the 21st century can be. It has come of age through the determination of a few committed individuals, rather than from anything very organised. It has happened in the hearts and minds of individuals. Its roots are in small human-scale concerns over waste, injustice, carelessness and a recognition of the need to live lightly in harmony with nature; it has come about in spite of government and the large concentrations of power. It has proved the power of individual will to change society, the power of spirit to move mountains. Above all, it has opened up the possibility that caring about things, looking beyond the short-term imperatives of growth and responding to the demands of natural justice are not incompatible with economics and marketing strategies.

GREEN WORK

We work for the planet when we apply ourselves whole-heartedly to living our vision, contributing our energy positively to the grand plan. In doing so, we come into relationship with our environment. As long as our impact is beneficial and sensitive, we are on the side of the angels.

Recycling paper, using lead-free petrol, careful sourcing (e.g. timber) and energy conservation are all good things to do and valuable as campaign themes. They are often a first point of contact for people new to green thinking. But we need to go very much further and deeper. We need to use very much *less* paper, detergent, petrol and timber, and manufacturers need to encourage us to buy less product. We need to keep our cars longer or, if possible, to do without them altogether. Instead of trading in the television, hi-fi, fridge, cooker, bed, furnishings, clothes and so on every 3 to 5 years, we need to think in terms of buying things to keep for 30 to 50 years, thus replacing production with repair and recycling.

When purchasing we should, whenever possible, buy locally-produced goods and food, which have a lower energy input because they have not travelled so far. And vegetarianism or, better still, vegan eating is a necessary trend because protein from meat is 10 times more expensive to produce than protein from cereals or legumes.

We must recycle buildings too, putting old industrial buildings to new uses, and only building new when every single building within 10 miles is fully utilised. Throughout, we must occupy only what we really need, whether as families or companies.

These are all areas where individual people and companies can have an impact. Notice how quickly attitudes can change once there is a will: look at the changed attitudes to fur coats, wearing seatbelts and smoking in public places. Attitudes to these have reversed in 10 years. The same is possible in environmental thinking.

Even when everything that can be done on the material level has already been done, we still have a long way to go. A product (or service or company) is only green when it creates a space in which all its employees can grow emotionally and spiritually, as well as financially and mentally. Denying the human spirit through hierarchical management structures, arrangements that interfere with customer relations, unequal distribution of power and ownership, and failing to provide outlets for creativity and self-esteem denies a company any claim to be green, holistic or ethical.

We must work responsibly and with integrity if we are to be good planetary citizens.

Holistic balance

It is all a matter of finding a balance between our ambitions and our responsibilities. You have found this balance when:

- you ask for what you want and not for more than you absolutely need;
- you believe you deserve to be abundant and not more abundant than anyone else;
- you use time and resources efficiently and are not mean with your time and resources;
- you are a good custodian and not obsessive about appearances;
- you charge the full going rate and are flexible to people's circumstances;
- you allow for a profit and distribute your profits for the common wealth;
- you embrace professionalism as well as the grace of God in your work.

A CODE OF ETHICS

An excellent statement of this balance at work in business is the Code of Ethics drawn up by the Findhorn Bay Business Network in Scotland. We would all do well to subscribe to it.

Findhorn Bay Business Network Code of Ethics

Individual integrity and alignment

Members maintain high standards of personal integrity. Members value and seek to embody the attributes of honesty, caring, spirituality and straightforwardness. Members seek to demonstrate rather than talk about these qualities. Members acknowledge that intuition and connection with a higher source are tools which should be used together with active communication among co-workers and customers to ensure that business becomes right livelihood.

Professional competence

Members take pride in their work and strive to provide excellent products and services to their customers and give value for money. Members aim to create products and services that leave both parties with a feeling of satisfaction and of mutual benefit.

Personal accountability

Members take full responsibility for the goods and services they provide and seek to express their personal values through their work. Members try to strike a balance between their personal needs and values and those of their customers.

Quality of working life

Members aim to create working environments where the individual is respected, supported and valued. The working environment should be a 'clear space' where the task of providing a quality service is paramount. Methods and tools such as conflict resolution and 'attunement' are used to create this clear space.

An atmosphere of trust allows delegation and empowerment

to become the normal way of working and allows each individual to contribute to their full potential.

Ownership
Members recognise that attachment to ownership can often hinder the full participation of co-workers and owners and are actively looking at ways to create more equitable and fulfilling business structures, while still recognising the validity of tried and proven structures.

Social responsibility
Members strive to use their skills and occupations to contribute to the quality of life and environment for all beings on this planet. Members attempt to create win/win situations in all of their relationships.

Global awareness
Members understand that the Earth has limited resources and are committed to maintaining a healthy productive planet. They aim to take responsibility for the environmental effects of their business activities. Members are conscious of the principle that sustainable businesses are developed to satisfy genuine needs.

The Findhorn Bay Business Network is run by Judith Meynell, Minton House, Findhorn, Moray. Judith also manages an on-going programme of training and development for companies entitled 'The Spirit of Business', which is at the forefront of the new consciousness in training for companies.

THE FIFTH COLUMN

We have no shortage of role models now, of people who have marched to the sound of a different drum. It becomes safer and safer, more and more normal to follow that inner voice.

How are *you* doing? How are your perceptions shifting? This might be a good moment to return to Chapter 2 and fill in the fifth column in the self-assessment questionnaire. The fifth column scores the impact of your belief systems when you are in touch with your inner voice, self-empowered and hopeful for yourself and humanity. It is also a measure of how far you may have shifted by reading this book and allowing abundance to flow. Join the fifth column! Change society from the inside.

How do you do this? How do you take your inner work into the messy domain of politics and business? Let's give the final word to Eileen Caddy, co-founder of the Findhorn Foundation in Scotland. At the end of their conference in October 1990, on intuitive leadership, Eileen presented a picture of how to introduce these ideas more widely. She drew a simple analogy.

'Don't try and take a dirty, worn-out old toy away from a child,' she said. 'It loves that old rag and will resist violently. Just put the new toy in alongside it. It may be rejected or thrown out. Just offer it again ... and again ... and again. Then when the child tires of its dirty old toy, the new one is there to replace it, already familiar and safe to turn to.

'You can't force people to change, and you don't have to. They are hungry for love and intuition.'

If not us, who?
If not here, where?
If not now, when?
If not through truth and love, how?

Wherever you are is a good place to start.

Bibliography

This book list includes books I have drawn on and quoted, and books that have been significant in my own development. Wherever possible I have also included books by people whose lectures, workshops or taped materials I have quoted.

Assagioli, Roberto *Psychosynthesis* Turnstone Press, 1965
Berne, Eric *Games People Play* Penguin, 1964
Blanchard, Kenneth/Johnson, Spencer *The One Minute Manager* William Morrow, 1982
Bloom, William *Meditation in a Changing World* Gothic Image, 1987
Bradley, Marion *The Mists of Avalon* Sphere, 1983
Caddy, Eileen *Foundations of A Spiritual Community* Findhorn Press, 1978; *Opening Doors Within* Findhorn Press, 1987; *Flight into Freedom* Element, 1988
Clark, Jonathan *The Barefoot Accountant* Brewin, 1990
Damian-Knight, Guy *The I Ching on Business and Decision Making* Century, 1986
Dass, Ram *Journey of Awakening* Bantam, 1978
Dass, Ram/Gorman *How Can I Help? − Emotional Support and Spiritual Inspiration for those who love* Century, 1989
Dauncey, Guy *After the Crash* Green Print, 1988
de Bono, Edward *Opportunities* Penguin, 1978
Eisler, Riane *The Chalice and The Blade* Harper & Row, 1987

Ferguson, Marilyn *The Aquarian Conspiracy* Routledge and Kegan Paul, 1981

Fromm, Erich *To Have or To Be* Abacus, 1978

Gibran, Kahlil *The Prophet* Heinemann, 1926

Handy, Charles *Future of Work: A Guide to a Changing Society* Blackwell, 1984; *Waiting for the Mountain to Move: And Other Reflections on Life*, Arrow, 1992

Harland, Maddy/Finn, Glen *Healthy Business* Hyden House, 1990

Harris, Thomas *I'm OK – You're OK* Pan, 1970

Heider, John *The Tao of Leadership* Wildwood House, 1985

Hill, Napoleon *Think and Grow Rich* Wilshire, 1937

Hills, Christopher *Nuclear Evolution* University of the Trees, Boulder Creek, 1977

Icke, David *It Doesn't Have To Be Like This: Green Politics Explained* Green Print, 1990

Inglis, Mary/Kramer, Sandra (ed.) *The New Economic Agenda*, Findhorn Press, 1985

Jampolsky, Gerry *Love is Letting Go of Fear* Celestial Arts, 1979

Kinsman, Francis *Millennium 2000* W.H. Allen, 1990

Lessem, Ronnie *Enterprise Development* Gower, 1986; *Developmental Management: Principles of Holistic Business*, Blackwell, 1990

Miller, Harley & Cally *Quality Cards* Hill Crest Enterprises, 1984

Moss, Richard *The I That Is We* Celestial Arts, 1981; *The Black Butterfly* Celestial Arts, 1987

Murray, W.H. *The Scottish Himalayan Expedition* J.H. Dent, 1951

Naisbitt, John *Megatrends* Futura, 1984

Peck, Scott *The Road Less Travelled* Hutchinson, 1978

Russell, Peter *The White Hole in Time* Aquarian/Thorsons, 1992

Sheehy, Gail *Pathfinders* Bantam, 1981

Spangler, David *The Laws of Manifestation* Findhorn Pubs., 1975

Spangler et al, *Reimagination of the World: Critique of the New Age, Science and Popular Culture* Bear & Co, USA, 1991

Toffler, Alvin *The Third Wave* Pan, 1980

Trevelyan, George *Vision of The Aquarian Age* Coventure, 1977; *Aquarian Redemption* Gateway, 1991

Wilhelm, Richard *I Ching (translation)* Routledge and Kegan Paul, 1951

Some of these are now out of print. Libraries and specialist bookshops with second-hand sections may be able to help.

Specialist bookshops include:

Watkins
19 – 21 Cecil Court
London WC2N 4EZ
071-836 2182

Quest Books
River House
46 Lea Road
Waltham Abbey
Essex EN9 1AJ
0992 88771

Compendium Books
234 Camden High Street
London NW1
071-267 1525

Index

THE BREAKTHROUGH CENTRE

WORKING FOR YOURSELF?

- **Running your own holistic enterprise?**
- **Freelance, part-time, self-employed work?**
- **Personal growth in employment?**

If it is important to you to combine green, ethical, holistic values and personal growth with the work you do, the first place to go is **The Breakthrough Centre.**

Founded in 1988 by Andrew Ferguson, author of *Creating Abundance*, the Centre is a physical focal point for those taking responsibility for their lives through self-employment and other personal growth routes. It provides:

- a wide choice of workshops on business, relationship and personal issues;

- The Breakthrough Club, a thriving network of holistic enterprise, offering telephone helplines, networking and massive discounts on Centre services;

- Findhorn Foundation and other visiting workshop leaders in London;

- free monthly sharing and meditation, open to all;

- training and counselling services to centres and companies of all sizes.

FOR DETAILS OF CURRENT PROGRAMME
Call **THE BREAKTHROUGH TEAM** on
081-749 8525
(International: +44 81 749 8525)
The Breakthrough Centre
7 Poplar Mews, Uxbridge Road, Shepherds Bush,
London W12 7JS, England

Piatkus Books

If you have enjoyed reading this book, you may be interested in other titles published by Piatkus.

BUSINESS AND SELF-EMPLOYMENT

Better Business Writing   Maryann V Piotrowski
Be Your Own PR Expert   Bill Penn
The Complete Time Management System   Christian Godefroy
Confident Decision Making   J Edward Russo and Paul J H Schoemaker
Creating Customers   David H Bangs
Dealing with Difficult People   Roberta Cava
How to Collect the Money You Are Owed   Malcolm Bird
How to Develop and Profit from Your Creative Powers   Michael LeBoeuf
How to Succeed in Network Marketing   Leonard S Hawkins
Lure the Tiger Out of the Mountains: *How to apply the 36 stratagems of Ancient China to the modern world*   Gao Yuan
Making Profits   Malcolm Bird
Marketing Yourself: *How to sell yourself and get the jobs you've always wanted*   Dorothy Leeds
Memory Booster   Robert W Finkel
Networking and Mentoring: *A woman's guide*   Dr Lily M Segerman-Peck
Organise Yourself   Ronni Eisenberg with Kate Kelly
Sales Power: *The Silva Mind Method for sales professionals*   José Silva

MIND, BODY AND SPIRIT

Care of the Soul: *How to add depth and meaning to your everyday life*   Thomas Moore
Colour Your Life: *Discover your true personality through The Colour Reflection Reading*   Howard and Dorothy Sun
Dare to Connect: *How to create confidence, trust and loving relationships*   Dr Susan Jeffers

Living Magically   Gill Edwards

Psycho-Regression: *A system for healing and personal growth*   Dr Francesca Rossetti

The Three Minute Meditator   David Harp

HEALTH

The Alexander Technique   Liz Hodgkinson

Be Your Own Best Friend: *How to achieve greater self-esteem and happiness*   Louis Proto

The Encyclopedia of Alternative Health Care   Kristin Olsen

Healing Breakthroughs: *How your attitudes and beliefs can affect your health*   Dr Larry Dossey

Increase Your Energy   Louis Proto

Nervous Breakdown: *What is it? What causes it? Who will help?*   Jenny Cozens

Self-Healing: *How to use your mind to heal your body*   Louis Proto

Super Health: *How to control your body's natural defences*   Christian Godefroy

Super Massage   Gordon Inkeles

For a free brochure with further information on our full range of titles, please write to:

Piatkus Books
Freepost 7 (WD 4505)
London W1E 4EZ

PIATKUS

THE COMPLETE TIME MANAGEMENT SYSTEM
by Christian H. Godefroy and John Clark

The Complete Time Management System will change the way you work and think. It will increase your enjoyment of life and your chances of success. It will show you:

- How to do in 2 hours what you usually need 4 hours to do
- How to revive your concentration
- How to read 240 pages an hour
- How to make an important decision faster
- How to delegate
- How to organise your office
- How to shorten meetings
- And much, much more

Learn the secrets of time management and you will profit from them all your life.

Christian Godefroy is a training specialist, founder of a publishing company in France and a best-selling author.

HOW TO COLLECT THE MONEY YOU ARE OWED
by Malcolm Bird

Getting paid on time is vital for any business. In *How to Collect the Money You Are Owed*, Malcolm Bird gives practical advice on how to organise your invoicing and money collecting systems, improve your cash flow and increase your profitability.

- Learn how to control your cash flow cycle
- Develop an efficient invoicing system
- Get to know your clients and how they operate
- Learn how to chase up money effectively
- Discover what to do if all else fails

How to Collect the Money You Are Owed will help you save time and money. It is an essential handbook for every office.

Malcolm Bird is a management consultant and author of several business books.

CARE OF THE SOUL
by Thomas Moore

Care of the Soul offers a new way of thinking about daily life – its problems and its creative opportunities.

- It offers a therapeutic programme for bringing the soul and spirituality back into your life
- It helps you to look more deeply into emotional problems and sense sacredness in ordinary things – real friends, satisfying conversation and fulfilling work

Care of the Soul is an inspirational guide that examines the connections between spirituality and the problems of individuals and society.

Thomas Moore is a Jungian psychotherapist, lecturer and writer.

LIVING MAGICALLY
by Gill Edwards

Living Magically is a lively and original introduction to the ideas, tools and techniques of metaphysics. In a practical, self-help way it will show you how to:

- Rediscover your inner wisdom and power
- Break through your fears, blockages and limitations and let go of the past
- Clarify your personal and global visions
- Listen to the 'whispers' from your Higher Self
- Make your dreams come true

Gill Edwards is a writer, clinical psychologist, therapist and workshop facilitator. She runs *Living Magically* workshops and is a practising metaphysician.